Behavioral
Consultation in
Applied Settings
An Individual Guide

APPLIED CLINICAL PSYCHOLOGY

Series Editors:
Alan S. Bellack, *Medical College of Pennsylvania at EPPI, Philadelphia, Pennsylvania,*
and Michel Hersen, *University of Pittsburgh, Pittsburgh, Pennsylvania*

Current Volumes in this Series

THE AIDS HEALTH CRISIS
Psychological and Social Interventions
  Jeffrey A. Kelly and Janet S. St. Lawrence

BEHAVIORAL CONSULTATION AND THERAPY
  John R. Bergan and Thomas R. Kratochwill

BEHAVIORAL CONSULTATION IN APPLIED SETTINGS
An Individual Guide
  Thomas R. Kratochwill and John R. Bergan

HANDBOOK OF BEHAVIOR MODIFICATION
WITH THE MENTALLY RETARDED
Second Edition
  Edited by Johnny L. Matson

HANDBOOK OF THE BRIEF PSYCHOTHERAPIES
  Edited by Richard A. Wells and Vincent J. Giannetti

HANDBOOK OF CLINICAL BEHAVIORAL PEDIATRICS
  Edited by Alan M. Gross and Ronald S. Drabman

HANDBOOK OF SEXUAL ASSAULT
Issues, Theories, and Treatment of the Offender
  Edited by W. L. Marshall, D. R. Laws, and H. E. Barbaree

HANDBOOK OF TREATMENT APPROACHES IN CHILDHOOD
PSYCHOPATHOLOGY
  Edited by Johnny L. Matson

PSYCHOLOGY
A Behavioral Overview
  Alan Poling, Henry Schlinger, Stephen Starin, and Elbert Blakely

---

A Continuation Order Plan is available for this series. A continuation order will bring delivery
of each new volume immediately upon publication. Volumes are billed only upon actual ship-
ment. For further information please contact the publisher.

Behavioral Consultation in Applied Settings

An Individual Guide

Thomas R. Kratochwill
University of Wisconsin–Madison
Madison, Wisconsin

and

John R. Bergan
University of Arizona
Tucson, Arizona

Plenum Press • New York and London

Library of Congress Cataloging-in-Publication Data

Kratochwill, Thomas R.
    Behavioral consultation in applied settings : an individual guide
  / Thomas R. Kratochwill and John R. Bergan.
      p.   cm. -- (Applied clinical psychology)
    Includes bibliographical references.
    ISBN 0-306-43346-X
    1. Mental health consultation. 2. Behavioral assessment.
  I. Bergan, John R., 1931-   . II. Title. III. Series.
    [DNLM: 1. Behavior Therapy--methods--programmed instruction.
  2. Consultants--education--programmed instruction. 3. Problem
  Solving--programmed instruction.   WM 18 K89b]
  RA790.95.K73 1990
  616.89'142--dc20
  DNLM/DLC
  for Library of Congress   89-26558
                                                             CIP

© 1990 Plenum Press, New York
A Division of Plenum Publishing Corporation
233 Spring Street, New York, N.Y. 10013

Printed in the United States of America

Preface

This guidebook has been developed as a skill-training package to teach psychologists, counselors, social workers, and other applied-mental-health professionals a model for the delivery of behavioral interventions through a behavioral consultation approach. This training guide is an abridged version of the skills taught as part of a behavioral consultation model. As such it is not intended to be an exhaustive program in behavioral consultation. Usually, consultation skills are taught over a period of several months in university training programs. *Also, the most successful use of the guidebook can be accomplished only with prerequisite training in behavioral analysis and assessment as a method of delivering psychological services.* Thus, individuals using this guidebook should obtain supervised training in this area. The book is also designed to accompany Bergan and Kratochwill (1990).

Some individuals may have a background in behavioral assessment and intervention. In this case, the use of this guidebook can provide the user who has not been exposed to the specifics of the behavioral consultation approach valuable information regarding interviewing forms of assessment and intervention. Such activities can be extremely useful when incorporated into regular clinical work in applied settings and supplemented with other assessment and intervention methods. Given the importance of successful interviewing in applied settings, a major clinical tool should be available after careful study of this guidebook.

To use this guidebook most effectively, it is recommended that the professional read the entire manual before implementing any of the procedures. It is also important to complete the self-quizzes at the end of each chapter. In each case, answers have been provided for the questions. Flexibility in the wording of responses is acceptable if the general content is correct. Various discussion questions have also been presented in the event that a group format is used for training purposes. In addition, it should be emphasized that a growing number of empirical investigations have been published that have a bearing on the scientific merit of the consultation approach. A select sample of some of these reports has been referenced along with the general sources on consultation. Individuals who wish to extend their knowledge in the consultation area will find these studies of much relevance.

Finally, any applied work must be implemented within the context of the ethical guidelines of the profession involved. Individuals working in applied settings in the delivery of mental health services should consult the ethical guidelines that have been developed for their profession. We have also included the guidelines from the Association for Advancement of Behavior Therapy (see Table 1.2 in Chapter 1) for those individuals unfamiliar with this code. Individuals unfamiliar with these guidelines should study them carefully and consider their implications for the practice of behavioral consultation. Moreover, individuals are advised to review the behavior therapy literature that outlines the major legal and ethical considerations in behavioral approaches to assessment and treatment (e.g., Schwizgabel & Schwizgabel, 1980; Stolz & Associates, 1978). It is our hope that acquisition of the consultation skills covered in the guidebook will improve the quality of psychological services and ultimately the lives of individuals receiving such services.

Acknowledgments

This guidebook was developed over a period of several years and went through numerous revisions during that time. We especially appreciate the feedback and recommendations from Daniel J. Reschly and Mark R. Shinn. We also offer appreciation to our students at the University of Wisconsin–Madison and the University of Arizona for their helpful comments on this work. A special note of thanks goes to Pamela Carrington Rotto, Susan Sheridan, and Kurt R. Van Someren for assistance in the training research that helped to improve the guidebook, and to Lynette Fassbender for her input on the guidebook. We also appreciate Karen Kraemer's assistance on this project.

Contents

1

Behavioral Consultation: An Overview

─────────────────── *Objectives* ───────────────────

This chapter provides an overview of behavioral consultation. On completion of the chapter the reader should be able to:

1. State the four defining characteristics of behavioral consultation.
2. Define the roles of the consultant, the consultee, and the client in behavioral consultation.
3. State three broad goals of behavioral consultation.
4. Describe the major differences between developmental and problem-centered consultation.
5. Describe and state an example of an operational definition.
6. Name and describe the four stages of consultative problem-solving.

Introduction

Consultation research, theory, and practice have expanded rapidly over the past decade. Increasingly, individuals working in applied settings have begun to adopt various aspects of consultation practice as conceptualized in the psychological literature. There is no one specific definition of consultation. In fact, the term *consultation* is used in many different ways throughout the psychological and educational literature. However, there are several different theoretical and applied models of consultation that occupy a prominent role in psychology and education. Each of these models provides a conceptual definition for practice in the area. Specifically, 10 different consultation models have been identified (West & Idol, 1987). However, in psychological practice in the schools, three major models are used most often: mental health consultation, organizational development consultation, and behavioral consultation. These models differ in theoretical orientation, consultative relationship, nature of the problem, consultation goals, and intervention methods, as well as the conceptual and methodological criteria used to evaluate the effectiveness of consultation (Reschly, 1976). (Table 1.1 provides the reader with an overview of various dimensions of the 10 consultation models.) The three most common are briefly reviewed.

17

TABLE 1.1. Analysis of 10 Consultation Models in Response to Five Criterial Questions[a]

Consultation model	Theory for the consultation relationship	Knowledge base for problem solving	Goals	Stages/steps	Responsibilities
Mental health (Caplan, 1970; Meyers et al., 1979)	Assumes that consultees have the capacity to solve most of their work problems and that consultants can help them increase their range of effectiveness (Gallessich, 1982). Theories that have been applied to how the consultant treats the consultee include neo-client-centered psychology (Rogers, 1942, 1951, 1959) and Adlerian psychology (Adler, 1964; Dreikurs, 1948, 1967). No single theory of communication has been applied.	Psychodynamics; clinical skills; crisis concepts; specialized diagnostic and decision-making skills; theme interference reduction; one-downmanship; avoidance of therapy; relationship building.	Consultant chooses one of four possibilities: client-centered, consultee-centered, program-centered, and administrative- or consultee-centered. Success is measured by the degree to which the consultation expands the consultee's capacity to diagnose, cope with, and solve emotional or technical problems of the consultee or the client.	Consultant chooses type of consultation for the problem and primary target of interventions. *Example:* 1. Consultant seeks information on nature and scope of work problem, consultee's capacity for problem solving, and ways the consultation might be useful. 2. Consultant "treats" the consultee by offering expert opinion, or shared, straightforward problem-solving is used.	Consultant is responsible for gathering information on the nature of the problem and for providing solutions to problems. The consultant–consultee relationship is egalitarian (Gallessich, 1985).
Behavioral (Bergan & Tombari, 1975,	Assumes that consultant's application of	Flexible knowledge of behavioral program-	To reduce the frequency of an unde-	1. Problems identification	Consultant serves as an expert; consultee

1976; Kratochwill & Bergan, 1978; McNamara & Diehl, 1974; Tombari & Bergan, 1978)	behavioral and social learning theory will help consultee solve problems. Behavioral learning theory has been more consistently applied to methods for problem solving than to how the consultant interacts with the consultee, although the latter would also be applicable.	ming and principles of social learning theory and applied behavior analysis.	sirable client–consultee behavior; to increase the frequency of desirable client–consultee behavior.	2. Problem analysis 3. Plan implementation 4. Problem evaluation (Bergan, 1977)	is the recipient although sometimes mutuality of problem solving is emphasized.
Organizational A. Human relations model (Argyris, 1964; Bennis, 1969, 1970; Homans, 1950; Lippitt, 1969)	Organizational theory: Problems of organizations must be solved in a manner that incorporates into the process all those individuals in the organization because of the focus that they bring to bear on one another (Lewin, 1951); the influence of environment on personal growth (Rogers, 1942, 1951, 1959).	Communication skills; decision-making skills; force-field analysis approved, data collection and feedback, social-psychological, cognitive behaviorism, ecology, psychodynamic systems, statistical models and methods, humanistic values and assumptions (Gallessich, 1983).	To bring about planned change by focusing on individuals and their attitudes and values and group processes in the organization (Brown et al., 1979); to increase organizational productivity and morale (Gallessich, 1982).	1. Orientation 2. Contract setting 3. Reconnaissance 4. Problem and opportunity development 5. Aspirations 6. Analysis 7. Experimentation 8. Results analysis 9. Program design 10. Implementation 11. Evaluation and feedback 12. Recycling (Gardner, 1974)	Consultant facilitates the group's progression through all stages.

(continued)

TABLE 1.1. (*Continued*)

Consultation model	Theory for the consultation relationship	Knowledge base for problem solving	Goals	Stages/steps	Responsibilities
B. Organizational thinking (Schmuck & Runkel, 1972)	Same as for the human relations model.	Group conflict, inter- and intragroup communication, decision making, methods of goal setting, defining roles.	1. Working with subsystems of the organization as groups 2. Developing communication skills 3. Working with subsystems to develop problem-solving skills 4. Developing a series of training exercises, which start with simulation and evolve to a point where the real issues of the school are the focus (Schmuck & Runkel, 1972)	1. Entry phase 2. Diagnosis of organization's functioning 3. Selection of a subsystem of the organization 4. Demonstration of the intervention (Brown et al., 1979) 5. Organizational training	Consultant facilitates process, demonstrates interventions, and provides training.
C. Advocacy	Any practitioners of other models may use advocacy consultation; based on conflict theory (i.e.,	Knowledge of law, organizing people, organizing events, media use, negotiation, parent part-	To seek due process for various types of clients; to facilitate group process to help people work to-	*None specified.*	Consultant facilitates effectiveness of others.

	Chesler, Bryant, & Crowfoot, 1981).	nership, persuasive writing and speaking, building support networks, tolerance for ambiguity and conflict; known for what they believe in *not* by particular methodologies. Some advocacy consultants have both expert content knowledge and advocacy process knowledge (Conoley & Conoley, 1982).	gether; to organize events; to develop partnerships with parents of clients.		
Process (Schein, 1969)	Systems change theory (von Bertalanffy, 1950).	Understanding of process phenomena; process observation, interaction analysis; decision-making rules data gathering; role identification; use of empirical approaches; reference for the unique (Conoley & Conoley, 1982; Neel, 1981).	Consultants work to make consultees more aware of events or processes that affect work production and social emotional atmospheres of the system (Schein, 1969); to leave a consultee (organization) with new skills (Conoley & Conoley, 1982).	1. Process observation 2. Analysis of group interactions	Consultant analyzes interactions of the group or organization; consultant and consultee work collaboratively to identify problems and to generate solutions; consultee provides information on organizational structure, climate, norms.

(continued)

TABLE 1.1. (*Continued*)

Consultation model	Theory for the consultation relationship	Knowledge base for problem solving	Goals	Stages/steps	Responsibilities
Clinical (doctor–patient)	The general characteristic is that it is patterned after psychiatry and adapted for use when consulting with colleagues about clients' problems. *No specified theory.*	Specialized expertise concerning the client's problem; expert power; referent power based on specialized expertise.	Expert diagnosis of a client's mental or emotional condition and an authoritative recommendation as to how staff (consultees) should treat the patient (Gallessich, 1982); problems are conceived of as patient's (or program's, team's, organization's) problems; generally goals are limited to the particular case; to increase consultees' coping effectiveness.	1. Diagnosis 2. Prescription 3. Treatment	Consultant assumes responsibility for the case, determines data to be gathered and how to gather them, directly examines client, treats or prescribes treatment; consultant–consultee relationship is hierarchical.
Program	*No specified theory.*	Methods are difficult to define because of the diversity in the nature of the consultation (Gallessich, 1982).	To help agencies design, develop, implement, and evaluate programs.	*Example:* 1. Consultee clarifies goals and objectives. 2. Consultant proposes ideal, theoretical	Consultants may assist in all aspects of the program or may be limited to a highly specific task.

Model	Theory	Education/training	Purpose	Stages or steps	Role of consultant
				approaches to objectives. 3. Consultee explains organizational constraints and resources. 4. Both "brainstorm" to develop practical implementation strategies. 5. Together develop a research and implementation plan. 6. Consultee implements the plan (Gallessich, 1982).	
Education/training	*No specified theory.*	Knowledge of open-systems operations; task analysis; needs assessment; instructional design; evaluation of training (Gallessich, 1982).	To transmit needed knowledge, information and skills to consultees to alleviate problems (usually client-centered).	*No specific stages or steps.*	Consultant serves as an expert.
Collaborative (Idol *et al.*, 1986; Kurpius & Robinson, 1978; Sarason, 1982)	Generic principles of collaboration and consultation have been hypothesized (Idol *et al.*, 1986);	Consultants possess knowledge of social learning theory, classroom assessment, learning pro-	To develop parity between special and classroom teachers resulting in shared ownership of learn-	1. Gaining mutual acceptance 2. Assessing causes of problems, problems themselves,	Emphasizes mutuality and parity in the consulting relationship with the consultant serving as

(continued)

TABLE 1.1. (*Continued*)

Consultation model	Theory for the consultation relationship	Knowledge base for problem solving	Goals	Stages/steps	Responsibilities
	based on triadic model of consultation (Tharp & Wetzel, 1969); no formal testing for theory development has been done.	cesses, child management, and applied behavior analysis; consultees possess knowledge of scope and sequence of curricular instruction, theories of child development, and techniques for large group instruction.	ing and management problems of exceptional and nonachieving students participating in regular classroom instruction.	and outcomes of problems 3. Formulating goals and objectives matched to assessment outcomes 4. Implementing teaching and learning procedures 5. Evaluating program outcomes including clients, consultants, consultees, parents of clients, program administrators, and overall programs (Idol *et al.*, 1986)	a learning specialist and the consultee serving as a curriculum and child development specialist; consultee is primarily responsible for program implementation; all other stages reflect mutual responsibility.

*a*From F. J. West and L. Idol (1987). School consultation: 1. An interdisciplinary perspective on theory, models, and research. *Journal of Learning Disabilities, 20,* 388–408.

Mental Health Consultation

Mental health consultation represents a widely used form of consultation in applied settings (Caplan, 1970; Meyers, Parsons, & Martin, 1979). This model of consultation has increasingly become diverse but generally embraces a more dynamic formulation of personality theory. Mental health consultation was developed with an emphasis on prevention rather than specific treatment of mental illness. With a shift during the 1960s toward community mental-health services and the reported failure of more traditional psychotherapy in treating emotional problems, mental health consultation focused on the prevention of more serious problems in community and school settings.

A major thrust for the development of mental health consultation was through the efforts of Caplan (1970) in his book *The Theory and Practice of Mental Health Consultation.* Contributions from this work first emphasized a coordinate relationship between professionals (e.g., psychologists and teachers). Second, Caplan addressed the consultation relationship and a variety of indirect techniques that can be used in the consultation process. Finally, he conceptualized consultation along the lines of a four-part categorization involving client-centered case consultation, program-centered administrative consultation, consultee-centered case consultation, and consultee-centered administrative consultation. A more comprehensive review of mental health consultation can be found in the work of Meyers and his associates (1979).

Organizational Development Consultation

The organizational-development consultation model has been used most extensively in industrial and organizational psychology. This approach has its theoretical heritage in the work of Kurt Lewin and, more recently, in social-psychological research on group processes. Organizational development consultation has also been used in educational settings.

Intervention procedures and techniques emanating from the organizational-development consultation approach involve such activities as group sessions to improve communication skills, to negotiate goals, and to reduce and resolve conflict and interpersonal relationships, among other group processes. The role of consultants in sessions is to facilitate development of these skills and activities, rather than to intervene directly in the organization. In keeping with this approach, a major goal of organizational development consultation is to establish a model for effecting self-change within the system to help the organization function more effectively with its members. Readers interested in this area are referred to some of the original literature on organizational development consultation (Schmuck, 1982; Schmuck & Miles, 1971).

Behavioral Consultation

Another major approach to consultation services in applied settings is based on behavioral consultation, which in turn is based on behavior-modification or behavior-therapy orientation (Kazdin, 1989; Sulzer-Azaroff & Mayer, 1977). To understand the behavioral consultation approach outlined in this guidebook, it is necessary to review briefly some of the perspectives on behavior therapy or modification.

Contemporary behavior therapy was developed, in part, as an alternative to the traditional and often unsuccessful psychological and educational practices in applied settings. Behavior therapy is not a unitary approach, and it is difficult to identify one central or defining core of contemporary practice. Kazdin and Hersen (1980) suggested the following major characteristics of the approach:

1. A strong commitment to empirical evaluation of treatment and intervention techniques;
2. A general belief that therapeutic experiences must provide opportunities to learn adaptive or prosocial behavior;
3. Specification of treatment in operational and hence, replicable terms;
4. Evaluation of treatment effects through multiple-response modalities, with particular emphasis on overt behavior. (p. 287)

As traditionally conceived, behavioral consultation involves indirect services to a client (e.g., a child) who is served through a consultee (e.g., a parent, or teacher), by a consultant (e.g., a psychologist, a special-education teacher, or a social worker). The use of behavioral procedures through a consultation approach requires a fundamental knowledge of behavioral psychology and its applications in practice. It also requires that individuals using the approach be able to translate this knowledge into practice. In this guidebook, we provide a brief review of the behavioral-consultation service-delivery model. It is essential that the individual have the prerequisite knowledge and skills in the area of behavior therapy or modification to profit from this manual. Clearly, the consultant must become familiar with the professional literature to acquire adequate knowledge of specific behavioral principles and strategies. The acquisition of specific knowledge must be accompanied by supervised applied case work with consultees and clients. Finally, it is essential that consultation practitioners adhere to the principles of ethical practice established for their specialty area of practice (e.g., the American Psychological Association or the National Association of School Psychologists). For the behaviorally oriented practitioner, the Association for the Advancement of Behavior Therapy has developed guidelines called "Ethical Issues for Human Services" (1977). These are reproduced in Table 1.2.

Providing services within the behavioral consultation model has several distinct positive features (Bergan & Kratochwill, 1990). One major feature is indirect service delivery in which a consultant works with a consultee who provides direct services to a client. For example, a consultant may provide services to a parent who is responsible for toilet training his or her child. The first major advantage of this indirect service approach is that consultation can have a broader impact than other forms of direct service. For example, when a consultant works directly with a child, other children in the family may not directly benefit from the intervention. On the other hand, when a professional works with a parent, the parent usually acquires skills that will assist in solving child-rearing problems that affect the functioning of the entire family.

A second advantage of behavioral consultation is that the consultant uses a problem-solving approach to the treatment of academic and social problems. The difficulties that clients bring to the attention of a consultant are defined and solved within the context of a problem or a set of problems. The emphasis is on determining what can be done about a given circumstance to improve existing conditions. The

TABLE 1.2.   Ethical Issues for Human Services[a]

The questions related to each issue have deliberately been cast in a general manner that applies to all types of interventions and not solely or specifically to the practice of behavior therapy. Issues directed specifically to behavior therapists might imply erroneously that behavior therapy was in some way more in need of ethical concern than non-behaviorally-oriented therapies.

In the list of issues, the term *client* is used to describe the person whose behavior is to be changed, *therapist* is used to describe the professional in charge of the intervention; *treatment* and *problem*, although used in the singular, refer to any and all treatments and problems being formulated with this checklist. The issues are formulated so as to be relevant across as many settings and populations as possible. Thus, they need to be qualified when someone other than the person whose behavior is to be changed is paying the therapist, or when that person's competence or the voluntary nature of that person's consent is questioned. For example, if the therapist has found that the client does not understand the goals or methods being considered, the therapist should substitute the client's guardian or another responsible person for *client*, when reviewing the issues below.

A. Have the goals of treatment been adequately considered?
   1. To ensure that the goals are explicit, are they written?
   2. Has the client's understanding of the goals been ensured by having the client restate them orally or in writing?
   3. Have the therapist and client agreed on the goals of therapy?
   4. Will serving the client's interests be contrary to the interests of other persons?
   5. Will serving the client's immediate interests be contrary to the client's long-term interest?
B. Has the choice of treatment methods been adequately considered?
   1. Does the published literature show the procedure to be the best one available for that problem?
   2. If no literature exists regarding the treatment method, is the method consistent with generally accepted practice?
   3. Has the client been told of alternative procedures that may be preferred by the client on the basis of significant differences in discomfort, treatment time, cost, or degree of demonstrated effectiveness?
   4. If treatment procedure is publicly, legally, or professionally controversial, has formal professional consultation been obtained, has the reaction of the affected segment of the public been adequately considered, and have the alternative treatment methods been more closely reexamined and reconsidered?
C. Is the client's participation voluntary?
   1. Have possible sources of coercion of the client's participation been considered?
   2. If treatment is legally mandated, has the available range of treatments and therapists been offered?
   3. Can the client withdraw from treatment without a penalty or financial loss that exceeds actual clinical costs?

TABLE 1.2.   (*Continued*)

D. When another person or an agency is empowered to arrange for therapy, have the interests of the subordinated client been sufficiently considered?
  1. Has the subordinated client been informed of the treatment objectives and participated in the choice of treatment procedures?
  2. Where the subordinated client's competence to decide is limited, has the client as well as the guardian participated in the treatment discussions to the extent that the client's abilities permit?
  3. If the interests of the subordinated person and the superordinate persons or agency conflict, have attempts been made to reduce the conflict by dealing with both interests?
E. Has the adequacy of treatment been evaluated?
  1. Have quantitative measures of the problem and its progress been obtained?
  2. Have the measures of the problem and its progress been made available to the client during treatment?
F. Has the confidentiality of the treatment relationship been protected?
  1. Has the client been told who has access to the records?
  2. Are records available only to authorized persons?
G. Does the therapist refer the clients to other therapists when necessary?
  1. If treatment is unsuccessful, is the client referred to other therapists?
  2. Has the client been told that, if she or he is dissatisfied with the treatment, referral will be made?
H. Is the therapist qualified to provide treatment?
  1. Has the therapist had training or experience in treating problems like the client's?
  2. If deficits exist in the therapist's qualifications, has the client been informed?
  3. If the therapist is not adequately qualified, is the client referred to other therapists, or has supervision by a qualified therapist been provided? Is the client informed of the supervisory relation?
  4. If the treatment is administered by mediators, have the mediators been adequately supervised by a qualified therapist?

---

[a]From: Association for Advancement of Behavior Therapy (1977). Ethical issues for human services. *Behavior Therapy, 8*, v–vi. Reproduced by permission.

problem-solving focus of consultation is consistent with the trend away from certain practices that emphasize the assessment of difficulties without formally attending to the task of establishing interventions to solve problems.

A third advantage of behavioral consultation involves the quality of the relationship between the consultant and the consultee. Consultation implies a collegial relationship. This type of relationship differs markedly from the patient–professional relationship associated with some traditional mental-health services. In the client–professional relationship, the client is often viewed as a patient and is regarded as suffering from a problem or disorder. In the consultation relationship, the consultant and the consultee are viewed as individuals, each with his or her own special expertise that can be applied to facilitate problem resolutions.

DEFINING CHARACTERISTICS OF CONSULTATION

A number of characteristics commonly associated with behavioral consultation are conceptualized as defining features. One of the most fundamental features of consultation is that the consultant uses problem-solving strategies to address the needs of the consultee and the client. Consultation typically involves an attempt to alter an existing set of problem circumstances in the direction of a desired set of circumstances. For example, a psychologist may be contacted by a teacher who is interested in learning how to manage the behavior of a specific child or children in the classroom. After defining the problem behavior(s) and identifying related variables, the consulting psychologist collaborates with the teacher to establish certain behavior-management strategies that will better equip the teacher with skills to help children. Careful application of the planned strategies potentially results in a more desirable classroom atmosphere.

Another feature of behavioral consultation is the indirect influence of the consultant on the client's behavior. Typically, the consultant does not have direct contact with the client during consultation; rather, the consultant works with the consultee, who, in turn, works with the client. The tactic of providing indirect services to clients has long been regarded as one of the most attractive features of consultation because the need for psychological services is far greater than the ability of society to provide such services. For example, the number of individuals who experience some form of psychological or psychiatric problems or difficulties in daily living and who could benefit from treatment has been estimated to be as high as 15%–25% in the United States (President's Commission on Mental Health, 1978). Consultation provides a tool that extends psychological and social services to many more individuals than could be served by direct contact with clients. By working with a consultee, such as a parent or teacher who is responsible for the socialization of several children, the skills learned through the consultation process may have benefits for other children, as well as for the referred child. Although indirect services is a major characteristic of consultation services, behavioral consultation does not always involve an indirect relationship between the consultant and the client. Often, it is necessary for the consultant to initiate direct contact with the client. This process occurs in several ways. For example, the consultant may work with the client to model various procedures for the consultee, who will eventually assume responsibility for the treatment. In addition, the client may have unique problems that require specialized treatment by the consultant. In such cases, it may be inappropriate for the consultee to provide treatment directly because of limited skills and training in the particular approach. Finally, services for the client may need to extend beyond treatment of client-specific problems in a single setting. For example, a teacher may be involved in the direct treatment of the child in the classroom, and the parents may pursue some form of family therapy simultaneously to deal with problems observed in the home setting.

A consultee may seek consultation services because he or she believes the consultant has pertinent knowledge and skills that will be useful. For this reason, one of the consultant's major responsibilities is to draw on his or her knowledge of behavioral psychology and consultation to make relevant information available to the consultee. To pursue this objective, the consultant must secure access to multiple resources to obtain the necessary information, must select specific principles and strategies for use in problem solving, and must communicate information clearly and concisely. These steps generally enhance the consultee's ability to apply specific methodology and potentially to improve the client's problem behavior(s). The consultant must study the problem thoroughly and must attempt to understand the teacher's perspective and numerous impinging variables (e.g., the classroom environment and the child's characteristics) to successfully collaborate with the teacher and effectively share knowledge and skills.

DEFINITION OF ROLES IN CONSULTATION

Three main roles associated with behavioral consultation involve the *consultant*, the *consultee*, and the *client*. It is the consultant's responsibility to understand thoroughly the stages in the consultation process (i.e., problem identification, problem analysis, and treatment evaluation) and to *guide the consultee through these steps*. The consultant accomplishes this largely by using a standardized interview format during the interaction with the consultee. A second role of the consultant during consultation is *to provide pertinent information and to make resources available to the consultee*. The consultant's knowledge is obtained from the empirical and applied literature in behavior therapy and other areas of psychology and education, as well as through applied experiences and practice.

Another important role of the consultant is less explicitly defined. The consultant generally does not exercise direct authority over the consultee, nor does the consultant establish a direct relationship with the client. However, it is the consultant's professional and ethical responsibility to see that the consultee *provides services that will benefit the client*.

The consultee is expected to engage in four kinds of activities during consultation. The first involves *specification and description*. As an initial step in the consultation process, the consultee usually describes a specific problem to the consultant. A second activity, which is invariably required of the consultee, is *evaluation or decision making*. Decisions such as those related to whether or not a satisfactory solution has been obtained for a particular problem generally rest with the consultee. A third kind of activity usually required of the consultee involves *working with the client* (i.e., implementing the intervention program). A final type of activity that a consultee may be expected to engage in is *supervision*. For example, the consultee may be called on to supervise the client's actions or those of assistants (e.g., paraprofessionals) who work with him or her in providing services to clients.

One of the special strengths of the behavioral consultation approach in the provision of psychological services is the fact that both the consultant and the consultee influence treatment implementation and outcomes. The interdependent contributions provided by the consultant and the consultee allow the client to benefit from the combined knowledge and skills of both professionals.

The client's primary role is to change in the direction of the goals established during consultation. In addition, the client may participate to varying degrees in *establishing the goals of consultation* and in *designing and implementing plans* to produce goal attainment.

GOALS OF CONSULTATION

The principal goal of consultation is to produce *change in client behavior*. Consultation for children and youths serving as clients may cover a broad range of behaviors involving both psychological and educational development. Moreover, the individuals providing services may develop preventive as well as remedial goals.

Consultation may also focus on *changing the consultee*. Goals associated with consultee change potentially include modification of individual knowledge or skills, change in confidence and ability to positively address client variables, and/or alteration in objective relations with the client. In some cases, the principle source of client difficulty may be the consultee. For example, a teacher may have inadequate skills and as a result may be unable to effectively manage children in the classroom. Furthermore, a change in the consultee may be beneficial for clients who are not directly involved in consultation. Thus, a teacher may acquire skills that will be applicable to a broad range of children in the classroom.

In addition to behavioral changes in clients and consultees, behavioral consultation sometimes focuses on producing change in the organization in which the client and consultee function (e.g., the school). The major goals that have been advanced with respect to organizational change fall into two broad categories: communication and problem solving. Communication goals deal with the effectiveness of communication among different components of an organization (e.g., communication between a teacher and a principal). Goals in the area of problem solving include encouraging consultees to develop pertinent skills and to apply these strategies with integrity. Thus, the consultant provides opportunities for the consultee to develop skills for defining problems, strategies for solving problems, and techniques for evaluating whether problem solutions have been attained. For example, an intervention frequently implemented in this area includes the provision of in-service workshops for either an entire school staff or a particular segment, such as the special-education faculty.

GOALS DEFINED IN BEHAVIORAL TERMS

Within the consultative problem-solving model, *the immediate goals of consultation are defined in behavioral terms.* In every case, consultation is aimed at producing clearly specified changes in behavior. To accomplish this, *operational definitions* are used to describe the behaviors of concern. In essence, an operational definition is a way of breaking down behaviors into observable and recordable events. For example, a child's aggressiveness may be defined operationally as an activity in which a child inflicts bodily damage or physical pain on another person (Fehrenbach & Thelen, 1982). The specific components of an operational definition and suggestions for developing a clear definition are described in Chapter 2 of this manual.

STAGES IN THE PROBLEM-SOLVING PROCESS

There are four stages in consultative problem solving: (1) problem identification; (2) problem analysis; (3) treatment implementation; and (4) treatment evaluation (see Figure 1.1). These sequential stages are the steps necessary to move from an initial designation of the problem of concern through the development and implementation of a plan designed to achieve problem solution. These stages also lead to the evaluation of goal attainment and plan effectiveness. The four phases overlap in actual practice as the consultant and consultee move toward successful resolution of the problem.

Problem Identification

Problem identification involves the *specification of the problem* or problems to be solved during consultation. Problem identification is

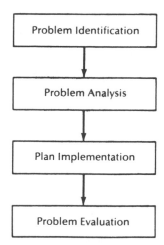

FIGURE 1.1. Stages of behavioral consultation.

achieved primarily by conducting a problem identification interview (PII). During the PII, the consultant assists the consultee in describing the problem of concern. After the consultee's concerns have been explored and defined in detail, the focus of the PII shifts to a discussion of the procedures to be used in measuring the baseline level of the behaviors targeted for change during the process of consultation. Problem identification is completed when the consultant and the consultee establish clearly that a discrepancy exists between the occurrence of the current and the desired levels of problem behavior. Methods for conducting the problem identification interview are reviewed in Chapter 2.

Problem Analysis

The primary purposes of the problem analysis stage are to *identify variables that might facilitate a problem solution* and *to develop a plan to solve the problem* previously specified in the problem identification phase. Problem analysis is accomplished through a problem analysis interview (PAI). During the PAI, the consultant and the consultee discuss client skills and/or environmental conditions that might influence client behavior. To this discussion, the consultant brings his or her knowledge of psychology and education and the consultee brings his or her knowledge of the child or student characteristics, familiarity with educational programs, and/or school, home, and community resources. Together, the consultant and the consultee share their professional or personal expertise and apply their knowledge to the specific situation. After hypotheses have been advanced regarding the kinds of factors that may influence client behavior, the discussion focuses on the development of a treatment plan designed to solve the problem. Clearly, behavioral consultation is intended to be perceived positively and to produce beneficial effects for all parties. However, consultees (e.g., parents or teachers) and behavioral consultants may occasionally have different reference points or perceptions of a problem (Rosenfield, 1985). It is therefore important that a consultant explore the consultee's conceptualization of the problem and examine some of the assumptions that guide a teacher's behavior in the classroom or a parent's behavior at home. If difficulties are experienced by the consultee as a result of knowledge deficits such as insufficient knowledge of theory, research, or techniques pertaining to the child's needs, the consultant may assume an educational role. This role involves sharing information to provide new and useful ideas that can be incorporated into the consultee's existing knowledge base and applied to intervention strategies used to change client behavior (Witt & Martens, 1988). Methods for establishing problem analysis are reviewed in Chapter 3.

Treatment Implementation

During the treatment implementation phase of consultation, the consultee implements or supervises the implementation of the plan designed during the problem analysis stage. Data collection continues as a source of information regarding the effectiveness of the plan. The consultant's central task during plan implementation is to ensure that the intervention is implemented with integrity. In other words, the consultee should use specific strategies as they were intended. To accomplish this, the consultant usually checks briefly with the consultee either by telephone or by direct observation. Methods for establishing treatments are reviewed in Chapter 4.

Treatment Evaluation

After a plan has been in effect for the designated period of time, problem evaluation is undertaken to determine the extent of plan effectiveness. Problem evaluation is conducted during a treatment evaluation interview (TEI). In the TEI, the consultant and the consultee determine whether problem solution has been achieved. This analysis is accomplished by comparing the data collected during plan implementation with the level of acceptable performance specified by the consultee in the problem identification interview. If the established goals have been attained, consultation may terminate. If the goals have not been achieved, behavioral consultation usually returns to problem analysis so that the original plan can be revised or a new one constructed. It is also advisable to evaluate the effectiveness of the treatment used during the implementation phase of consultation. The method of treatment evaluation depends on the measures that have been implemented to assess plan effectiveness. Methods for establishing a treatment evaluation are reviewed in Chapter 5.

TYPES OF CONSULTATIVE PROBLEM-SOLVING

There are two types of consultation problem-solving strategies: *problem-centered* and *developmental*. These two types of consultation approaches vary in several specific key features (see Table 1.3).

Problem-Centered Consultation

Problem-centered consultation calls for action related to a limited number of specific behaviors of immediate concern to the consultee, as in the case of decreasing the frequency of specific conduct problems of a child in the classroom. In the case of problem-centered consultation, it is the consultant's task, at least initially, to address the more immediate problems that the consultee presents.

Developmental Consultation

Developmental consultation is concerned with changes in behavior that require a relatively long time to treat. For example, general

Table 1.3.   Key Features of Consultation Problem-Solving

Key features	Consultation types	
	Problem-centered	Developmental
Nature of problem	Specific target behaviors	Interrelated target problems; disorders
Focus of treatment	Specific treatment techniques aimed at target problems of client	Combination of treatment of client, teacher, and family possible
Time of consultation process	Brief time period	Relatively long time period
Consultation objectives	Specific performance objectives	General objectives and subordinate and performance objectives
Consultation process	Single application of PII, PAI, and TEI	Repeated applications of PII, PAI, and TEI

improvement of social interactions in a child requires a considerable amount of time. The focus of developmental consultation is invariably on the attainment of one or more long-range goals. Moreover, the achievement of each of these long-range goals generally requires the mastery of subordinate objectives that are hierarchically related to the long-range goals. These various subordinate objectives would, of course, be developed to meet the needs of one particular child through reiterative applications of consultation within that particular context.

Developmental consultation generally requires repeated applications of the consultative problem-solving model. Consultation may focus initially on one or two specific behaviors related to a given subordinate objective. All phases of the problem-solving process would be implemented in an effort to achieve the goals established with respect to these behaviors. Following goal attainment, other behaviors related to subordinate objectives would be targeted for change. Reiterative applications of the problem-solving process would continue until all of the objectives of the developmental consultation are achieved.

APPENDIX A
Self-Quiz

EXAMPLE 1

During an interview conducted with a teacher, the consultant and the teacher (the consultee) identified the temper tantrums of a first-grade child as the problem of concern. They defined tantrums as crying and lying on the floor for longer than 3 minutes at any one time.

    a. This probably takes place during a _____

    _____ interview.

    b. "Crying for longer than 3 minutes at any one time" is part of

    an _____ _____ of the problem.

EXAMPLE 2

During problem identification, the long-range objective identified by the parent was to reduce his son's fear reactions. The achievement of this goal was accomplished by breaking the problem down into a number of subordinate objectives, such as minimizing the fear of interacting with other children and minimizing the fear of going to school.

    c. This is an example of _____ consultation.
    d. Achievement of the goal to reduce the child's fear reactions

    will require _____ applications of the problem-solving process.

EXAMPLE 3

A child is throwing temper tantrums every night at bedtime and her parents wish that she would never throw a temper tantrum.

    e. The discrepancy between the temper tantrums occurring at bedtime and the fact that her parents want *no* temper tantrums constitutes the _____ identified in this interview.

f. The plan devised to remedy this situation will take place dur-

ing a _____ _____ interview.

EXAMPLE 4

Based on the recommendation of the consultant, a mother re-duced the frequency of her children's arguments by turning off the TV whenever her son and daughter started to argue about which show to watch. She did this very matter-of-factly and stopped talking at length with them about how to solve their disagreements.

g. In this case, change in the clients' behaviors was effected by a

change in _____ _____.

h. This took place during the _____ _____ phase of consultation.

EXAMPLE 5

"Since our goal of eliminating Bob's hitting has been only par-tially attained, we need to understand further the conditions that might be controlling the occurrence of Bob's aggressive acts."

i. This statement probably was spoken by the _____

during a _____ _____ interview.

j. Determination of whether or not the goal had been attained

was probably accomplished by comparing _____

_____ before and after plan implementation.

APPENDIX B

Quiz Answers

a. problem identification
b. operational definition
c. developmental
d. reiterative or repeated
e. problem
f. problem analysis
g. consultee behavior
h. treatment implementation
i. consultant, treatment evaluation
j. data collected

Appendix C
Reading Quiz

1. Consultation typically involves an attempt to alter

    (a) _____ in the direction of

    (b) _____ .

2. Consultation usually involves a _____ relation-
    ship between the consultant and the consultee.

3. The three main roles in consultation are

    (a) _____ , (b) _____ , and

    (c) _____ .

4. It is the _____ responsibility to establish the
    stages in the consultation process.

5. The consultant's role is to _____ .

6. The client's role is to _____

    _____ .

7. The principal goal of consultation is to produce _____

    _____ .

8. The immediate goals of consultation are defined in _____

    _____ .

9. An _____ _____ is a way of
    breaking down behaviors into observable and recordable
    events.

10. _____ _____ calls for action re-
    garding a limited number of specific behaviors of immediate
    concern.

11. The four stages in consultative problem-solving are

    (a) _____ .

(b) _____ .

(c) _____ .

(d) _____ .

12. A problem is defined as _____

_____ .

13. The purpose of _____ _____ is to
identify variables that may facilitate the achievement of a
problem solution and to develop a plan to solve the problem
specified.

APPENDIX D
Reading Quiz Answers

1. (a) an existing set of circumstances
   (b) a desired set of circumstances.
2. collegial
3. (a) consultant
   (b) consultee
   (c) client.
4. consultant's
5. guide the consultee through the consultation process and to
   provide pertinent information and resources.
6. change in the direction of the goal.
7. a change in client behavior.
8. behavioral terms.
9. operational definition
10. problem-centered consultation
11. (a) problem identification.
    (b) problem analysis.
    (c) treatment implementation.
    (d) treatment evaluation.
12. the discrepancy between observed behavior and desired
    behavior.
13. problem analysis.

APPENDIX E

Discussion Questions

The following questions are designed to elicit further considerations in consultation models of service delivery. The questions are to be used to promote group discussion following Chapter 1.

1. What model or model of consultation does the reader affiliate with in practice?
2. What are some of the system barriers that are related to establishing a consultation service delivery model?
3. What are some of the advantages and limitations of the use of behavior modification procedures in applied settings?
4. What type of intervenion programs can be used in applied settings without major restructuring of the systems in which they are implemented?
5. What type of childhood problems are suitable for problem-centered and developmental consultation?

2

Problem Identification

———————— *Objectives* ————————

On completion of this chapter the reader should be able to:

1. Name the five steps in problem identification.
2. Name five characteristics or objectives in behavioral consultation.
3. Name and describe three specificity levels for objectives.
4. Name and describe three types of measures of client performance.
5. State six important questions to be answered about data collection procedures in behavioral consultation.
6. Name three types of objectives to be achieved during the problem identification interview.
7. Compare and contrast problem identification procedures for developmental and problem-centered consultation.

INTRODUCTION

Problem identification is the first step in the consultation problem-solving process. Problem identification plays a particularly critical role in consultation because it potentially results in the design and implementation of an effective plan. If the problem is not identified correctly, the plan may be ineffective or it may not meet the needs of the situation.

It is important to emphasize that the problem identification phase of consultation generally occurs when the consultant initiates the first personal contact with the consultee. The consultee must be afforded the highest respect and regard. The consultant should note that he or she is providing consultation services to assist both the consultee and the client. Every effort must be made to promote a good working professional relationship between the consultant and the consultee in this context. Various interpersonal relationship variables affect the entire consultation process and should be carefully considered.

THE PROBLEM IDENTIFICATION PROCESS

The problem identification process consists of a series of steps designed to lead toward the specification and definition of the problems described by the consultee during the consultation interaction. The steps in the structured interview eventually result in the designation of the goal or goals to be achieved through consultation, the measurement of current client performance with respect to whatever goals are to be attained, and an assessment of the discrepancy between existing client performance and desired client performance. The outcome of behavioral consultation is thought to be successful when the discrepancy between existing performance and desired performance is eliminated.

The problem identification phase includes the following steps: (1) establishing objectives; (2) selecting measure of client performance; (3) collecting data; (4) displaying data; and (5) defining the problem by assessing the discrepancy between the current performance and the desired performance objectives as reflected in the data collected.

Establishing the Objectives

The first step in the problem identification process is to initiate a specification of the goal or goals to be achieved through consultation. Objectives have numerous characteristics, including (1) the specification of the kind of activity required to achieve the objective(s); (2) an indication of the level of performance required for attainment of the objective(s); (3) a specification of the individual or individuals for whom the objective(s) is intended; (4) designation of the conditions under which performance of the objective(s) is to occur; and (5) a deadline for achieving the specified objective(s).

Objectives vary widely in specificity. Objectives representing the broadest level of performance are called *general objectives*. Objectives of moderate specificity related to general objectives are called *subordinate objectives*. The most specific objectives are called *performance objectives*.

The most significant function served by the general objective is to provide an organizational framework within which to conceptualize other goals. This organizational framework helps to ensure the development of objectives that are coordinated for the attainment of an overall goal. Other functions of the general objective include the provision of a long-term focus for goals and the reduction of the number of objectives an individual must consider.

A general objective implies the attainment of all the goals within a given category of objectives. A general objective encompasses all of the subordinate and performance objectives of concern to the participants in behavioral consultation. General objectives are therefore defined by their relation to other goals that have been specified. They normally include only a broad description of the kinds of activities required for goal attainment and the level of required performance. Moreover, there is no designation of the conditions under which performance is to occur or the deadline within which the objective must be attained. An example of a general objective would be for a client to achieve "confidence" in specified social situations.

Subcategories associated with a given general objective are referred to as *subordinate objectives*. Several hierarchically related levels of subordinate objectives may be associated with a general objective. Subordinate objectives, like general objectives, are expressed in rather broad terms. They do not usually contain a precise designation of activity type or required performance level, and they generally do not include a specification of conditions or deadlines. Like general objectives, subordinate objectives provide a broad classification within which a number of subclassifications may be grouped; they offer a relatively long-range focus in goal specification, and they reduce the number of objectives that must be kept in mind in situations calling for goal specification.

One unique function of subordinate objectives is linking performance objectives to general objectives. The use of hierarchically arranged categories of subordinate objectives makes it possible to link large sets of performance objectives into logical sequences. Sequencing of this nature not only serves the important function of specifying the relationship between objectives in an area, but it also provides guidelines for establishing and prioritizing the specific sets of performance objectives to be targeted in consultative problem-solving. An example of a subordinate objective formulated under the general objective of "achieving confidence in social situations" might be that the client display less verbal self-criticism.

The most specific type of objective is the performance or behavioral objective. The three defining characteristics of a performance objective are (1) a behavioral description of the activity desired; (2) the specification of performance conditions; and (3) a precise indication of the required performance level. A behavioral description specifies in observable terms the actions to be taken toward the accomplishment of an objective. The description must be sufficiently explicit so that independent observers can agree on whether an individual has performed the actions required by the objective. Table 2.1 describes the criteria for well-conceptualized behavioral definitions. Examples of operational definitions are given in Table 2.2.

One function of the performance objective is to provide a specific focus for goal-directed activities. It is vital that the consultant and the consultee focus their attention and efforts on the achievement of specific, mutually agreed-upon goals. A second function of the performance objective is to relate the goals to performance measures. When an objective is stated in terms of desired performance, it is usually relatively easy to devise a method for measuring the attainment of the objective. A third function of the performance objective is to facilitate goal attainment. Many investigators have noted that behavioral objectives may enhance learning and thereby promote the achievement of socialization and academic goals. An example of a performance objective specified under the subordinate objective of "displaying less verbal self-criticism" would be that the client completely stop making self-critical comments at home, in informal social gatherings with friends, and with teachers. The most commonly observed self-critical

TABLE 2.1.   Some Criteria for a Good Operational Definition[a,b]

1. The definition should be *objective*, referring only to observable characteristics of the behavior (and environment, if needed) or translating any inferential terms (such as "expressing hostile feelings," "intended to help," or "showing interest in") into more objective ones.
2. The definition should be *clear* in that it should be readable and unambiguous so that experienced observers could read it and readily paraphrase it accurately.
3. The definition should be *complete*, delineating the "boundaries" of what is to be included as an instance of the response and what is to be excluded, thereby directing the observers in all situations that are likely to occur and leaving little to their judgment.

[a]A list of definitions may be found in L. Litow (1977). *Glossary of classroom behaviors*. Abstracted in the *Journal Supplement Abstract Service Catalog of Selected Documents*, 7(2), 53. Available from the American Psychological Association, Document #MS1492.
[b]"Criteria for Behavioral Definitions" from R. P. Hawkins & R. W. Dobes (1977). Behavioral definitions in applied behavior analysis: Explicit or implicit? In B. C. Etzel, J. M. LeBlanc, & D. M. Baer (Eds.), *New developments in behavioral research: Theory, method, and application*. Hillsdale, NJ: Erlbaum.

TABLE 2.2. Some Examples of Operational Definitions of Target Behaviors

Target behavior(s)	Operational definition

Teacher behaviors

Purpose: These behaviors are intended to reflect the kind and amount of attention the teacher directs toward the children in his or her classroom. When used in conjunction with the child behaviors, scoring reflects the kind of child behavior that the teacher attends to, and in what ways.

Positive (+)

Purpose: This category is intended to reflect the amount of attention the teacher uses that children usually like. Clearly, the attention that each child finds reinforcing is different; it is hoped that this category will include the kinds of teacher attention that most children like.

Definition: (1) All verbal praise to an individual child, such as "Good," "That's nice," "I like that," "Wonderful," and "Great." Verbal statements in this category are usually marked by strong emphasis in tone of voice. Obviously, teachers may lower their volume if they do not want to disturb other children who are working.

(2) All "warm" physical contact, including hugs, kisses, pats on the head, and enveloping contact (e.g., putting an arm around a child). Excludes incidental touching and contact that is not enveloping (e.g., putting an arm on the shoulder of a child).

(3) Dispensing of food or other tangible reinforcers, including points, toys, tokens, and individual time with the teacher (if designated as a reinforcer). This also includes teacher statements indicating that a reinforcer is being dispensed (e.g., "You may watch television now").

Negative (−)

Purpose: This category is intended to reflect the kind of teacher attention that children generally do not like.

Definition: (1) All verbal reprimands, such as "No!," "Stop!," "I don't like that," "Is that the way to act?" or "Do we do that in this room?" Statements in the form of questions, such as "Did you leave the blocks out?" (which clearly implies, "You should not leave the blocks out") should be coded as negative (−). Excludes feedback that an answer is incorrect, if not marked by strong intonation.

(2) Aversive physical contact, including restraints, yanks, jerks, pulls, pushes, slaps, hits, pinches, and arm dragging. Excludes rough physical contact that occurs as part of an activity (e.g., being hit with a ball during play, or accidental aversive physical contact).

(3) Time out, exclusion from activities, being sent out of a room, and point fines.

(4) Statements of negative consequences: "Keep that up and you're out!" or "Get out."

Attention (A)

Purpose: This category should reflect attention that a child receives that is of a relatively neutral quality, and that cannot be scored in one of the other categories.

Definition: (1) Smiles, frowns, prolonged gazes (when the observer is sure of what the teacher is looking at), looking over a child's shoulder, and nonenveloping touches (e.g., hand resting on shoulder).

(continued)

TABLE 2.2.   (*Continued*)

Target behavior(s)	Operational definition

(2) Other neutral attention, such as irrelevant conversation or use of the child's name.

(*NOTE*: Score "A" only if none of the other teacher behaviors are observed in that same interval in which the "A" occurs.)

Child behaviors

Question answering

Participation (P)

Saying an answer regardless of the question asked (may be similar to speaking out but is task-relevant; score as "S" if teacher reprimands or discourages this behavior).

Volunteering for tasks or chores (e.g., cleaning up)

Asking for work to do

Talk *about* task to class

(*NOTE*: Score "P" only if these behaviors occur in a *group setting*, which is more than two class-member children.)

On-task (T)

Looking at a book

Looking at parent during discussions

Doing what told to do (compliance)

Writing in book or on paper (task-related)

Reading (to oneself)

Disruptive motor

Behavior (D)

Hitting, kicking, pushing, shoving, pinching other family members

Destroying property

Throwing objects

Slamming doors

Pushing tables or chairs (includes moving a chair around when not given directions to do so)

Speaking out (S)

Irrelevant and usually distracting to both the child and others

Off-task comments

Swearing

Name calling

Whispering to other children

Talking to oneself

Noise (N): Mouth noises, screeches, howls, whoops, whistles, or cat calls comments made by the client should then be specified to increased the operational applications of this performance objective.

As noted in Chapter 1, consultative problem-solving may focus on the achievement of long-range developmental goals (developmental consultation) or on specific problems of immediate concern (problem-centered consultation). These focal differences require variations in the problem-solving process. One of the major differences between developmental and problem-centered consultation involves the specification of objectives. Developmental consultation requires the establishment of general, subordinate, and performance objectives. General and subordinate objectives are designated first, and performance objectives are specified later. In the initial problem-identification effort, only a limited number of performance goals are identified. These objectives are then pursued through consultative problem-solving. Provisions are also made for the formulation of additional performance goals in reiterative applications of the problem-solving process.

In problem-centered consultation, general and subordinate objectives are not designated. Rather, discussion moves immediately to the specification of one or a limited number of behavioral goals that are of concern to the consultee. In the problem-centered approach, the consultant's first task is to elicit behavioral descriptions of those aspects of client functioning that are of concern to the consultee. In contrast, developmental consultation focuses on the description of the behavior desired for the client.

Problem-centered consultation differs from developmental consultation in the description of conditions as well as in the specification of behavior. The conditions specified in performance objectives in developmental consultation indicate the circumstances that must prevail during performance aimed at mastery of the objective. The description of conditions in problem-centered consultation establishes the circumstances under which the behaviors of concern are now occurring. The central purpose of describing conditions in problem-centered consultation is to identify environmental factors or stimulus conditions that may influence behavior. This definition also contributes to behavioral-consultation goal definition. As the consultant and the consultee explore the conditions under which the behavior occurs, they also specify the conditions under which it must occur for them to agree that the goals of consultation have been met.

Another difference between developmental and problem-centered behavioral goals involves the specification of required competency levels. In developmental consultation, the required competency level is generally established during the problem identification interview as part of the discussion of the performance objective under consideration. In problem-centered consultation, the designation of the competency level is usually deferred until after the collection of baseline data, so that the consultee has an opportunity to consider the client's current level of performance in making a decision concerning the desired level of performance. Generally, a discussion regarding the current strength of the client's behavior provides information about the severity of the problem, and it can be helpful in establishing procedures for subsequently assessing client performance.

Selecting Measures of Client Performance

The second step in problem identification is to select measures of client performance related to the goals of consultation. Three broad categories of measures are (1) standardized tests; (2) work samples; and (3) naturalistic observations.

Standardized tests used during the process of problem identification are intended to provide a measure of the current performance of the client with respect to the objectives to be achieved through consultation. The decision about whether a test should be used as a measure of client behavior during problem identification is based on the type of goal to be attained and the availability of an appropriate test to measure it. For example, if the consultee's objective is to reduce the number of disruptive behaviors occurring in the classroom, obviously a standardized testing approach to goal measurement would be inappropriate. On the other hand, if the objective is to increase accuracy in solving division problems, specific criterion-referenced or path-referenced testing of division would be a useful tool for assessing client behavior (see Bergan & Kratochwill, 1990, for a more detailed account of assessment strategies).

In educational settings, a convenient and accurate measure of client performance is work samples. Work samples provide objective evidence regarding client actions (because they are tangible products of client behavior); they require little or no effort on the part of the consultee; and they also afford the consultant an almost effortless opportunity to observe direct evidence of client behavior. The main disadvantage of work samples as a measure of client performance is simply that many objectives do not lend themselves to a work-sample format.

Perhaps the most widely used procedure for measuring client behavior during problem identification is direct observation of the behavior as it occurs in the natural environment of the client. The advantage of behavioral observations is that they relate easily to the objectives formulated in consultation.

Collecting Data

After measures have been selected for the assessment of client performance, data on client behavior must be collected. Data collection requires careful planning by the consultant and the consultee to determine answers to questions such as: What shall be recorded? How shall recording occur? How many data shall be collected? When shall recording take place? How many observations shall be made? Who shall do the recording?

Determining what to record is related to four behavioral characteristics frequently assessed by means of naturalistic observations: magnitude, latency, duration, and frequency of behavior. *Magnitude* refers to the amount of a response, such as how loudly a child speaks. Magnitude is sometimes discussed within the context of response quality, where both intensity (amplitude) and acceptability are considered important features (Hartmann, 1984). In the latter case, the consultant may be interested in qualitative features of the target response. *Latency of response* refers to the time period between the end of a stimulus and the onset of a response signaled by that stimulus (e.g., the time it takes a child to begin to follow an instruction given). *Duration* refers to the length of time that a behavior or set of behaviors occurs, such as the amount of time spent actually working on homework (on-task). Frequency data involve the number of times a particular behavior occurs, such as how many times a child asks a question in class.

The question of how to record observational data involves decisions regarding the appropriateness of a mechanical counter, a tape recorder, a specially designed form, or a simple piece of paper for recording the behavior observed. Regardless of the method used to collect data, the pertinent information often involves the time that a behavior occurred, the fact that it did occur, and the antecedent and consequent events related to it. It is not always necessary or useful to record all of these events, but this kind of information suggests some of the factors that may be influencing client behavior, and thus, it may be of particular value during problem analysis. Figure 2.1 provides an example of a recording form that may be used to conduct client observations.

Observational Strategies

When designing an observational assessment strategy, the consultant must consider the response characteristics to be observed. There are five basic approaches to recording behavior, which are used under specific circumstances: real-time observations, interval recording, scan sampling, event recording, and duration recording. Together, these procedures cover the majority of the situations encountered in behavioral consultation.

Real-Time Observations

These observations typically involve recording event frequency and/or duration in terms of their natural, ongoing occurrence.

Interval Recording

This procedure (also referred to as *time sampling*) provides an estimate of both the number of occurrences and the duration of a behavior. It is used to measure the presence or absence of behavior within specific time intervals. In other words, interval recording is a measure of the number of intervals within which the behavior is observed to occur. Interval recording is used when the behavior occurs at a moderate but steady rate. In the use of the interval method of recording, the observation period is broken into small, equal inter-

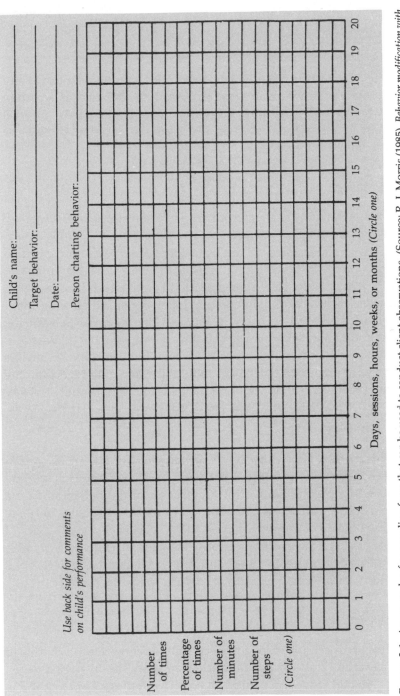

Child's name: _____
Target behavior: _____
Date: _____
Person charting behavior: _____

*Use back side for comments
on child's performance*

Number
of times

Percentage
of times

Number of
minutes

Number of
steps

(Circle one)

0 1 2 3 4 5 6 7 8 9 10 11 12 13 14 15 16 17 18 19 20

Days, sessions, hours, weeks, or months *(Circle one)*

FIGURE 2.1. An example of a recording form that can be used to conduct client observations. (Source: R. J. Morris (1985). *Behavior modification with exceptional children: A systematic guide.* Glenview, IL: Scott Foresman.)

vals, and the observer records whether the behavior is observed in each interval.

The two main types of interval recording are whole interval and partial interval. In whole interval recording, the behavior is recorded only when it occurs during the entire interval. In partial interval recording, a behavior is recorded if it occurs at any time during the predetermined interval.

Scan Sampling

This technique (also referred to as *instantaneous time sampling, momentary time sampling,* or *discontinuous-probe time sampling*) is a measure of the number of times the behavior is observed at prespecified sampling points in time (e.g., at the *end* of every 10-second interval, or at the end of every 15-minute period). In other words, the presence or absence of behaviors immediately following specified time intervals is recorded. This procedure requires the observer to scan the subject and to note whether the target response occurs at that instant. Momentary-time-sampling procedures may be used with behaviors that occur at moderate but steady rates and when data regarding the duration of the behavior are more meaningful than frequency data.

Event Recording

This method (also called *frequency recording,* or *trial* or *tally methods*) provides a tally or count of behaviors as they occur. This method measures the precise number of occurrences of the behavior during the entire observation session. Thus, event recording requires a specification of the exact number of times that a specific behavior occurs. It is appropriate for measuring responses that are discrete (with a clearly definable beginning and end) and is used when the frequency of a behavior is of interest.

Duration Recording

This approach provides a measure of the precise length of time of each instance of the behavior during an observation period (e.g., Tracy attended for a cumulative total of 23 minutes). This method is used in cases in which both numerical and temporal aspects of the behavior are essential. Duration recording may be relatively difficult because the observer must identify exactly when the behavior starts and stops. Because the extent of time of a behavior may be difficult to measure, duration recording is recommended only when the duration of the problem is of major concern.

Each method of observation has a number of advantages and limitations (see Table 2.3). For more detailed information on observational assessment, the reader should review some primary works in the area (Gelfand & Hartmann, 1984; Hartmann, 1984).

Considerations

Because of the well-known fact that behavior may change as a function of time, it is generally useful to take some precautions to ensure that the behavior observed during the problem identification phase will not simply be a transitory phenomenon. This problem is generally handled by collecting data over a series of points in time. A series of data points of this kind provides a baseline against which to judge changes that may occur as a result of treatment.

The first issue that should be considered in determining the length of baseline recording is the consistency of behavior. If the dimension of behavior being observed is highly stable across a number of occasions, then the period of collecting baseline data may be quite short. On the other hand, if the behavior is highly unstable, it is usually advisable to collect data over a longer period.

A second factor that must be considered in determining the length of the baseline is the amount of behavior under examination. Behavior that occurs at a very high rate need not be recorded for as long a period as low-rate behavior in order to yield reliable information regarding the extent of fluctuation.

A final factor related to the length of the baseline is the severity of the problem as judged by the consultee and/or the consultant. In the case of severe problems, it may be necessary to curtail or eliminate entirely the collection of baseline data.

In most cases, the consultee is responsible for recording client behavior. Depending on the circumstances, however, the client himself or herself, other individuals working with the consultee, or even

TABLE 2.3.   Factors to Consider in Selecting an Appropriate
Recording Technique[a]

Method	Advantages and disadvantages

Real-time recording
  Advantages
    Provides unbiased estimates of frequency and duration.
    Data capable of complex analyses such as conditional probability analysis.
    Data susceptible to sophisticated reliability analysis.
  Disadvantages
    Demanding task for observers.
    May require costly equipment.
    Requires responses to have clearly distinguishable beginnings and ends.
Event or duration recording
  Advantages
    Measures are of a fundamental response characteristic (i.e., frequency or duration).
    May be used by participant-observer (e.g., parents or teachers) with low rate responses.
  Disadvantages
    Requires responses to have clearly distinguishable beginnings and ends.
    Unless responses are located in real time (e.g., by dividing a session into brief recording intervals), some forms of reliability assessment may be impossible.
    May be difficult with multiple behaviors unless mechanical aids are available.
Momentary time samples
  Advantages
    Response duration of primary interest.
    Time saving and convenient.
    Useful with multiple behaviors and/or children.
    Applicable to responses without clear beginnings or ends.
  Disadvantages
    Unless samples are taken frequently, continuity of behavior may be lost.
    May miss most occurrences of brief, rare responses.
Interval recording
  Advantages
    Sensitive to both response frequency and duration.
    Applicable to a wide range of responses.
    Facilitates observer training and reliability assessments.
    Applicable to responses without clearly distinguishable beginnings and ends.
  Disadvantages
    Confounds frequency and duration.
    May under- or overestimate response frequency and duration.

[a]Adapted from D. M. Gelfand and D. P. Hartmann (1984). *Child behavior: Analysis and therapy* (2nd ed.). Elmsford, NY: Pergamon Press. Copyright 1984. Reproduced by permission.

the client's peers may be involved in data collection. It is generally not recommended that the consultant collect the data because it is not efficient use of his or her time. Although a consultant should not take the responsibility for data collection, this does not imply that he or she should not make an attempt to observe client behavior where this would be useful. Direct observation of a client by the consultant may be very helpful in making a more precise assessment of the problem situation and of the nature and scope of target problems as well as in directly observing the environmental variables that may be effecting the behavior.

Displaying the Data: The Graph

After data have been collected, they should be summarized in a form that may be interpreted easily. For several reasons, the line graph is the most common data-display technique used in consultation. First, line graphs provide a visual representation of the behavior under analysis. The visual information presented on a line graph is usually easier to comprehend than a similar amount of information presented verbally. Second, graphic display of the data may alert the consultant and the consultee to factors that influence the behaviors of concern in consultation, such as changes in the frequency of these behaviors. The interested reader is referred to Bergan and Kratochwill (1990) for additional information.

Defining the Problem

The visual display of data presented in graphic form provides the necessary information for problem definition. As indicated above, a problem is defined in terms of the discrepancy existing between observed performance and desired performance. In determining this discrepancy, it is important to consider both the magnitude of the difference between performance and objectives (i.e., shifts in the average rate of performance) and the trend in performance (i.e., systematic increases or decreases over time). The consultee must decide whether the discrepancy is of sufficient proportions to warrant a problem-solving effort.

THE PROBLEM IDENTIFICATION INTERVIEW

The problem identification process is initiated by means of the problem identification interview. During this interview, the consultant and the consultee collaboratively specify objectives to be achieved through consultation and determine procedures for measuring performance with respect to specific objectives. Three major objectives for problem identification are (1) goal specification; (2) assessment; and (3) procedural considerations.

Goal Specification Objectives for Developmental Consultation

In developmental consultation, the initial task of the consultant is to attain specification of the general, subordinate, and performance objectives. Such specification can be achieved in a single interview when the number of objectives is relatively small. However, when many objectives are involved, a number of interviews may be required.

During the earliest phases of problem identification, the aim of the consultant should be to establish the general and subordinate objectives. Little attention should be given to the hierarchical positioning of these objectives. Only after a list of fairly broad goals has been constructed should the focus of the problem identification interview(s) shift to the hierarchical classification of objectives. The goal at this stage of problem identification is to construct a complete classification system for the general and subordinate objectives. This system should specify the objectives to be achieved and the hierarchical relationship among them.

In the advanced stages of problem identification, the interview focus shifts to the establishment of performance objectives related to the various categories of subordinate objectives that have been designated previously. This process sometimes occurs over an extended period of time. The goal of each session conducted during this phase of the problem identification process is to establish a limited set of performance objectives that are to be the focus of consultee intervention efforts in the immediate future. This process enables the consultant and the consultee to effect changes in client behavior immediately.

Goal Specification Objectives for Problem-Centered Consultation

In problem-centered consultation, the consultant's first objective leading toward goal specification is to obtain a precise description of the behaviors of concern to the consultee. The designation of the goals to be achieved with respect to the behaviors of interest is deferred until later in consultation. The consultant initiates the behavior specification process by eliciting behavioral descriptions of the client's functioning from the consultee.

The goal of attaining behavioral descriptions from the consultee involves several factors. First, vague delineations of client actions are replaced by language describing precisely what the client does (i.e., in terms that are understandable to an independent observer). The consultant must also make sure that the behaviors described are, in fact, essential to the definition of the problem of concern. When a consultee is asked to describe client behavior, he or she often briefly mentions several behaviors, only some of which are really pertinent to the problem. Moreover, when behaviors that are significant from a problem-solving standpoint are mentioned, some of the actions described are of greater concern and relevance than others. For example, the mother of a 5-year-old child might say, "Tammy is such a messy eater at mealtimes, and she always leaves her toys all over the house. She really irritates me because she never does what I ask her to do." In a situation like this one, it is the consultant's task to guide the consultee to prioritize each of the behaviors described. Priorities may be used to determine which behaviors should be the immediate focus of problem-solving efforts.

After behavioral descriptions have been attained for those behaviors that are to be the immediate focus of treatment, the consultant's goals should be to obtain a description of the conditions under which these behaviors occur. This description should include the specification of related antecedent, consequent, and sequential conditions. Contextual variables should be considered as well (Donnellan, Mirenda, Mesaros, & Fassbender, 1984). Figure 2.2 provides the reader with a flowchart depicting an assessment strategy for forming hypotheses regarding the communicative functions of various behaviors, but it can also be useful in consultation for a wide range of client problems.

Antecedent conditions are events occurring immediately before

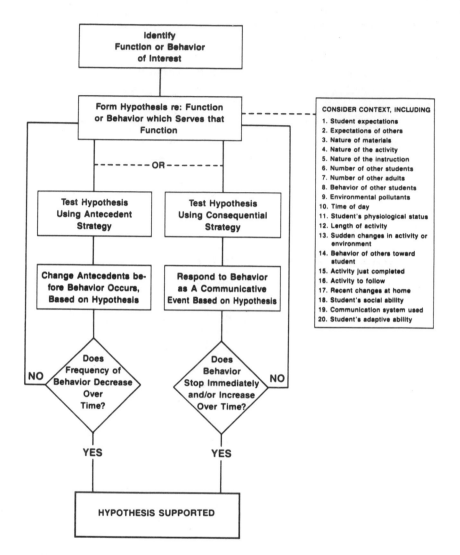

FIGURE 2.2. Analyzing the communicative functions of aberrant behavior. (Source: A. M. Donnellan, P. L. Mirenda, R. A. Mesaros, & L. L. Fassbender (1984). Analyzing the communicative functions of aberrant behavior. *Journal of the Association for the Severely Handicapped, 9,* 201–212.)

the child exhibits the target behavior that is being discussed by the consultant and the consultee. Consequent conditions are events that occur immediately after the client's behavior. Sequential conditions indicate the time of day or the day of the week when the behavior of concern typically occurs, or the pattern of antecedent and/or consequent conditions across a series of occasions. For example, a particular case of child noncompliance in the school may be found to present itself during the hours between 10:00 and 11:30 A.M. weekdays, and never in the afternoon. The specification of related conditions gives the consultant tentative information that can be used in problem analysis to determine environmental factors that may be influencing behavior. It can also be used to establish the conditions under which client performance must occur for the consultee to agree that the goals of consultation have been achieved. For example, consider the case of a high school teacher who is concerned about a group of female students who are smoking in the girls' lavatory. The teacher's immediate objective may be to stop the smoking in that location. The location then becomes a condition of goal attainment.

The final objective leading toward goal specification in problem-centered consultation is to elicit an indication of the level of incidence, or strength, of the specific target behavior(s). However, at this point, information regarding the occurrence of the behavior(s) is considered an approximation, as baseline data have not been collected. Nevertheless, a description of the behavior strength provides the consultant with some indication of the severity of the problem. Likewise, it is also useful for determining when to record occurrences of the behavior and subsequently for scheduling observation times. The consultant generally does not attempt to obtain specification of the desired incidence of behavior from the consultee until after baseline data have been collected.

Performance Assessment Objectives

The first interview objective related to the assessment of client performance is for the consultant and the consultee to mutually select the measure to be used to assess client behavior. The consultant may suggest the *kind of measure* that he or she believes to be most suitable for the consultee's needs and may then seek approval of the suggestion from the consultee. The consultee may also have applied knowledge or suggestions that he or she would like to discuss. It is essential that both parties agree on the particular measure.

The second performance-assessment objective during the problem identification interview is the specification of what will be recorded. The type of strength measure used in recording behavior must be agreed on. Although the consultant should assume responsibility for the assessment by suggesting a strength measure and seeking consultee agreement on it, the consultee may also wish to contribute related suggestions.

The other assessment goals to be achieved in the problem identification interview address the necessity of securing mutual agreement regarding (1) how data are to be recorded; (2) how much behavior is to be recorded; (3) the recording schedule; and (4) who is to collect the data. The consultant should assume leadership in the collaborative framework by addressing these considerations based on specific knowledge of the problem.

Procedural Objectives in Problem Identification

During each stage of the consultation process, a number of procedural details must be given attention. The first detail involves establishing the date and time for the next interview. The consultant should elicit a time when it would be most convenient for the consultee to meet again as determined by the limitations imposed by individual schedules. It is usually not advisable to allow more than a week to elapse between the interviews, although this may be contingent on the type and severity of the target problem. The collection of baseline data should generally be completed within 1 week. In most cases, waiting longer to collect the data and subsequently to schedule the next interview would unnecessarily delay problem solution.

A second procedural detail that should be handled during the problem identification interview is arranging to contact the consultee during the collection of the baseline data. The consultant must be certain that everything is going as planned. This procedure provides a safeguard against unfortunate consequences that may arise when a consultee has misunderstood specific procedures related to baseline data collection. Likewise, the consultant makes himself or herself available to address questions that may arise between consultation interviews.

A sample interview is included at the end of this chapter. It demonstrates the attainment of three major objectives from the problem identification interview: goal specification, assessment, and procedural considerations. In addition, several important verbal-interaction techniques are demonstrated. The reader should carefully study the procedures used by the consultant in this example to effectively achieve these objectives.

The behavioral consultant elicits specific kinds of information by guiding the consultee toward a discussion of the information needed to affect alterations in client behavior. As mentioned above, the behavioral approach encourages problem definition in behavioral terms. It is, therefore, the task of the behavioral consultant to work with the consultee in translating the often-ambiguous language of everyday speech into behavioral language. The importance of this clarification lies in the fact that everyday language is frequently vague and may not seem to refer to actual behavior. A parent may complain, for example, that his or her children are "driving me crazy," and that "they act as if they hate each other." Obviously, in such a case, the specific nature of the problem behaviors has yet to be operationalized by the consultant and the consultee.

A major goal of consultants is to specify behavior in sufficiently precise terms to ensure objective measurement. The precise specification of behavior is useful because it makes it possible for the consultant to interpret the consultee's evaluations of the client. For example, when a consultee says something like "Bob's immaturity really bothers me," the consultant is faced with the task of helping the consultee to specify precisely what is of concern. On the other hand, if the consultee says, "Bob's hitting really bothers me," the consultant gains a relatively specific understanding of at least one aspect of the client's actions that is important to the consultee.

Behavioral definitions are sometimes quite easy to formulate. For example, a father may report that this child cries too much when he puts him to bed at night. The behavioral consultant would help this consultee to formulate a statement that describes exactly what behavior is a problem. They might arrive at a definition that includes obnoxious, loud crying, while excluding talking and other soft noises made by the child. Thus, the consultant and the consultee may agree that a cry is any vocal noise produced by the child that is loud enough to be heard outside the child's room and that does not involve recognizable words. This description constitutes an operational definition because it tells both participants in the problem identification interview what should be defined as a "cry."

The formulation of a behavioral definition for crying is quite straightforward because the word itself refers to a well-understood behavior. Thus, the purpose of the definition is to clarify exactly what is to be considered a cry and what is not. However, there are many words used to discuss human behavior that are not this clear. For example, a teacher may complain of the "bad attitude" that one of his or her fourth-grade children exhibits. Although most of us would agree that the child must be doing something that annoys the teacher, it is almost impossible to guess what it is. In fact, it may be more than one thing. The term *bad attitude* doesn't begin to specify the behaviors that might be involved.

A consultant faced with a complaint about a child's bad attitude would have to question the teacher to obtain a more specific idea of his or her complaint. He or she might determine that the teacher doesn't like the fact that the child isn't studying very often, is obnoxious to friends, and is often rude. The consultant would not attempt to formulate a behavioral definition of the general term *bad attitude*. Rather, he or she might work to formulate with the consultee a definition of each behavior (lack of studying, obnoxiousness, and rudeness), or he or she might focus on only one of the behaviors, after determining the behavior of greatest concern to the consultee at the present time. In any event, a vague term such as *bad attitude* should be broken down into more precise *behavioral* terms defined as specifically as possible.

In addition to making objective observation possible, specifically defined behaviors facilitate clear communication. If the participants involved in consultation fail to break vague terms into more specific behavioral words, they may not be working on the same problem.

Another reason that behaviorally oriented consultants tend to be concerned with precise descriptions of client behavior is that these objective definitions make it possible to investigate environmental influences on the behavior of concern, as well as its antecedents, consequences, and sequential factors. Behavioral consultants view conditions within the immediate environment in which behavior occurs as major determinants of behavior. Accordingly, they are generally interested in obtaining information regarding all three of these conditions. Behavioral consultants are interested in antecedent conditions because they facilitate the identification of factors that potentially signal the occurrence of specific behaviors. For example, through questioning, a consultant might establish that a child's complaining behavior generally follows his or her parents' instructions to begin a new activity. The parents' instructions may serve as a signal for the child to complain.

The behavioral consultant must also determine consequent conditions to identify variables that may increase or maintain problem behaviors. Therefore, a consultant might ask the consultee what happens immediately after a particular behavior to identify possible controlling events. Sequential conditions provide the behaviorally oriented consultant acquiring information about variables such as sequential conditions that may affect the retention or response rate. (These behavior-influencing variables are discussed in more detail in Chapters 3 and 4.)

In addition to guiding the consultee toward providing useful behavioral information, it is the consultant's task to clarify and check the validity of what has been communicated. The consultant does this through summarization and validation. Throughout the interview, it is useful to frequently review the information discussed earlier within the interview or at a time before the interview. One obvious function of the summary is to enhance the consultee's recall of what has been said before. Participants in consultation say many things, and it is impossible to remember them all. The summary serves as a kind of rehearsal that restates previously discussed material and thereby reduces the probability that it will be forgotten.

In addition to facilitating recall, summaries may help to establish a focus in the interview. Summaries are invariably selective. They do not recount everything that has been said previously. Rather, the consultant selects those aspects that seem especially important.

Summarizing information periodically throughout each interview may also help the consultant and the consultee to arrive at a shared understanding. For example, summarization provides an opportunity for the consultant to explicitly state his or her understanding of the problem or situation. Likewise, it provides an opportunity for the consultee to endorse what has been stated or to indicate areas of difference between the two viewpoints. Thus, a final function of the summary is to review material that requires agreement between the consultant and the consultee. For example, the consultant and the consultee should agree about the plans developed to address the problem presented during the consultation interview. A validation should follow the summary, calling for agreement or disagreement with regard to what has been said.

The central function of validation in consultation is to establish a consensus between the consultant and the consultee as they move toward a shared understanding of the specific problem. Questions establishing this consensus should be stated so that they can be responded to with a "yes" or "no" response. For example, a consultant might say, "Am I correct in assuming that Alice cries only when she is put down for her nap?"

During problem identification, consensus achieved through validation is required to ensure agreement regarding the particular behaviors that concern the consultee, the conditions under which these behaviors occur, and the procedures established for recording behaviors.

The following examples of problem identification interviews should be read carefully. Note the use of the various verbal techniques described above.

PROBLEM-IDENTIFICATION-INTERVIEW EXAMPLES

Developmental Consultation

The first example presented in this chapter is a developmental problem identification interview. With respect to interview structure, developmental consultation differs from problem-centered consultation mainly in the manner in which the problem identification interview is conducted. The case to be presented below illustrates the use of the developmental approach in formulating goals for increasing the social competency of a second-grade girl.

The Problem Identification Interview

Consultant: (1) Jody, what are your general concerns regarding Candy's behavior? (2) In very general terms, tell me about her behavior.

Consultee: She is a very complicated child. She has had quite a difficult background. Mainly, I guess it's her adjustment to her new home, her adjustment to the new class situation, and being able to get along with her peer group.

Consultant: (3) Okay.

Consultee: All of these things are based on what has been happening to her in the past.

Consultant: (4) As far as adjustment to her classroom situation is concerned, what are some of the things you are talking about?

Consultee: Her behavior is inappropriate in that she has a hard time staying in her seat. She has a hard time knowing when to speak out and when not to. She does a lot of blurting out of things when she shouldn't. She has been taking things from other children; yet, she wants very much to be their friend and to be my friend.

Consultant: (5) The general area then appears to be of social nature, getting along with other children.

Consultee: Right. Rather than academics.

Consultant: (6) Academic behavior is not uppermost in your mind?

Consultee: She does quite well.

Consultant: (7) In the area of social concerns, it would be adjustment to the classroom situation, staying in the seat, speaking at appropriate times, and taking things from others that concern you about her social behavior.

Consultee: She just doesn't know how to go about getting along with other people. There are a lot of little things that happen that cause her not to be liked by the other children. Yet, they are trying, in part, to overlook things. She doesn't seem to be willing to try to work things out by herself nor does she seem to understand what is necessary. She just seems to go down her own little path.

Consultant: (8) So that the major goals that you have, or the directions that you would like to move in, are for her to be able to get along better with others and to adjust to the classroom situation better. (9) You see those as two separate areas: adjusting to the classroom and getting along better with others?

Consultee: Separate, yes. But it is important to work on them together.

Consultant: (10) As far as getting along better with others is concerned, what are some of the things you would like her to do?

Consultee: I would like her to learn to understand others. What are some of the necessary social skills she needs to have? She needs to know when children want to be her friend. She often puts the children in a position where she demands this friendship. When she doesn't get it, she turns kind of vengeful instead of trying to figure out what she is going to do in order to get them to be her friends.

Consultant: (11) Alright, she demands friendship. (12) What exactly does she do in these kinds of situations?

Consultee: When she is wanting to have friends?

Consultant: (13) Yes.

Consultee: She will pull at them physically, handle them in trying to get them away from other children. She often tries to give things to the children and then expects them to turn around and be her friends because she has given something to them. She tries to get up and be by a particular person at a time when she shouldn't be out of her seat. The other child knows what is going on is wrong and tries to ignore it or tells her to sit down or something. She still stays right there.

Consultant: (14) Then, in getting along with peers, it is to know when she is with friends not to demand their friendship or to get them away from other children or to try to bribe them into being her friends, but to understand the ways in which she can get other children to like her. (15) Is that right?

Consultee: Yes.

Consultant: (16) In the area of adjustment to the classroom, what are some of the skills that you would like her to have?

Consultee: I would like her to stay in her seat when it is the appropriate time to be in her seat. I would like her to listen when I say, "Please go sit down," rather than have to get to the point where I am having to get mad at her. I don't like to get to that point. She won't listen at first. She won't listen a second time, and so on. I would like her to raise her hand instead of just blurting out in class. These are the main things she needs to work on, I think.

Consultant: (17) Our two major areas of concern are getting along with other children and adjusting to the classroom situation. (18) Which of these areas would you want to concentrate on?

Consultee: I think working on the classroom behavior. I think that if that can begin to come around, the children would, in turn, understand and like her better.

Consultant: (19) Under classroom behavior, what do you want to work on first? (20) You mentioned staying in her seat, listening when spoken to, and raising her hand to be called on. (21) Which of those would you like to work on first?

Consultee: I would like to work on the one that I think we could remedy the fastest and easiest so that the other things could come around. So I would say following directions.

Consultant: (22) The situation we would like her to follow directions in is in the classroom. (23) Is there any particular time?

Consultee: During direct teaching time. (During the time that they do independent work.) I think it would be mostly when it is not teacher-directed.

Consultant: (24) So whenever you are doing direct teaching to the group you would like her to follow whatever directions you give to the group?

Consultee: No. Wait a minute. I think I want to change that. I would say, actually, that we have the most trouble in between subjects, while we are changing over, when we are changing the activity or something. That is when she has the hardest time.

Consultant: (25) So whenever you are changing from one activity to another and you give a direction to the class, you would like her to follow the direction immediately. (1) Would you be able in the next few days, until I get back here on Tuesday, to keep track of how many times you give a direction and it is not followed by her? (2) It could simply be just keeping a running tally during those times.

Consultee: Shall I keep track of specifically what the direction is?

Consultant: (3) If you can, because there may be one type of direction that she is not following rather than another. (4) The type of directions and whether or not she follows them would be a simple thing. (5) Record every time you give one and whether or not she follows it so we have a percentage.

Consultee: Okay. Sure.

Consultant: (6) Then our goal is to get her to adjust to the classroom, (7) and our first step is to get her to follow directions. (8) Once we have helped that, we can concentrate on staying in her seat and that sort of thing.

Consultee: I think that is good.

Consultant: (9) Can we get together, then, next Tuesday, look at the data, and go from there?

Consultee: Yes. This same time?

Consultant: (10) Fine. (11) Thanks.

Discussion of the Interview Transcript

The interview can be examined from a number of perspectives. We prefer to discuss it within the context of the Consultation-Analysis

Record (CAR) presented in Bergan and Kratochwill (1990). The CAR shown in Figure 2.3 reveals that the consultant in this case was, for the most part, effective in the use of the content, process, and control message-classification categories. As is appropriate, the content of the consultant's verbalizations was limited largely to the subcategories of behavior, behavior setting, and observation. In accordance with the expectations of a developmental interview, the largest number of utterances was in the behavior subcategory. Verbalizations in this content area reflected the consultant's efforts to establish general, subordinate, and performance objectives in the case. Utterances in the behavior-setting subcategory dealt with establishing the conditions under which performance had to occur to satisfy the requirements of the objective of following directions, which was the goal selected to be the initial focus in consultation. Verbalizations in the observation subcategory had to do with establishing procedures for collecting baseline data. There probably should have been more utterances in both the behavior-setting and the observation subcategories. It would have been useful to have additional information about the specific kinds of situations in which following directions was expected to occur. In addition, it would have been helpful to have more information regarding how recording was to occur.

The consultant was effective in his use of the process category as well as the content category. Verbalizations fell mainly in the specification, summarization, and validation subcategories. This distribution is the general pattern desired in behavioral consultation. However, there should have been a more equal distribution across process subcategories. Specifications far outweighed summarizations and validations.

The consultant's use of the control category was adequate, and his use of elicitors provided control of the interview. He was able to engage the consultee in discussion of a large number of topics by using elicitors to gain information and by restricting his use of emitters to summarization.

There were a number of specific things the consultant said that produced beneficial outcomes in the interview. First of all, he focused the interview by attempting to elicit general objectives from the teacher. The first question, "What are your general concerns regarding Candy's behavior?" helped the consultant to generate information about the problem. After eliciting general goals from the consultee,

CONSULTANT __Milton__   CASE NUMBER __1__

CONSULTEE __Jody__   INTERVIEW TYPE __PII__

PAGE __1__

CONSULTATION-ANALYSIS RECORD

	Message Source		Message Content							Message Process							Message Control	
	Consultee	Consultant	Background Environment	Behavior Setting	Behavior	Individual Characteristics	Observation	Plan	Other	Negative Evaluation	Positive Evaluation	Inference	Specification	Summarization	Negative Validation	Positive Validation	Elicitor	Emitter
1	/				/								/				/	
2	/				/								/				/	
3	/				/											/		/
4	/				/								/				/	
5	/				/							/						/
6	/				/											/	/	
7	/				/									/				/
8	/				/									/				/
9	/				/											/	/	
10	/				/								/				/	
11	/				/									/				/
12	/				/								/				/	
13	/				/											/		/
14	/				/									/				/
15	/				/											/	/	
16	/				/								/				/	
17	/				/									/				/
18	/				/								/				/	
19	/				/								/				/	
20	/				/									/				/
21	/				/								/				/	
22	/		/										/					/
23	/		/										/				/	
24	/				/											/	/	
25	/				/									/				/

FIGURE 2.3. Message classification analysis of consultant verbalizations in a developmental problem-identification interview.

CONSULTANT __Milton__   CASE NUMBER __1__

CONSULTEE __Jody__   INTERVIEW TYPE __PII__

PAGE __2__

CONSULTATION-ANALYSIS RECORD

	Message Source		Message Content							Message Process							Message Control	
	Consultee	Consultant	Background Environment	Behavior Setting	Behavior	Individual Characteristics	Observation	Plan	Other	Negative Evaluation	Positive Evaluation	Inference	Specification	Summarization	Negative Validation	Positive Validation	Elicitor	Emitter
1		/					/						/				/	
2		/					/						/					/
3		/					/									/		/
4		/					/					/						/
5		/					/						/				/	
6		/			/									/				/
7		/			/									/				/
8		/			/								/					/
9		/							/							/	/	
10		/							/							/		/
11		/							/			/						/
12																		
13																		
14																		
15																		
16																		
17																		
18																		
19																		
20																		
21																		
22																		
23																		
24																		
25																		

FIGURE 2.3. (*continued*)

he attempted to link the previously established general objectives to subordinate goals. For example, in an effort to establish subordinate objectives, the consultant remarked, "As far as adjustment to her classroom situation is concerned, what are some of the things you are talking about?" A little later in the interview he asked, "As far as getting along better with others is concerned, what are some of the things you would like her to do?"

When the subordinate objectives were established, the consultant provided further focus by asking the consultee to select a particular goal as an initial focus for the purposes of consultation. At this point, the consultee responded unexpectedly in the interview. She selected following directions in the classroom as the objective of primary concern. This choice was an objective that had not been specifically mentioned previously in the interview. To define following directions in performance terms, the consultant should have used an elicitor such as "What would Candy have to do to demonstrate that she was following directions?" The consultant might also have said, "Give me some examples of the ways in which Candy could show that she was following directions." Questions such as these would have increased the likelihood of agreement between the consultant and the teacher regarding what was meant by the phrase "following directions." The questions could also have had a beneficial influence on the accuracy of baseline recording in that they would have assisted the consultee to specify in a precise way the particular behaviors to be recorded. Finally, questions calling for a behavioral specification of following directions could have helped to set the stage for an examination in problem analysis of the conditions related to following directions. In the absence of a clear specification of the term "following directions," the consultant might have asked a question such as "How did you react when Candy did not follow a direction?" A question of this kind would probably yield less information than a question such as "What did you say to Candy when she failed to start working on her math problems after you had told her to do so?" To ask a question of the latter type, the consultant needed to elicit a behavioral description of the term *following directions*.

The major strength displayed by the consultant while conducting the problem identification interview was her ability to elicit information from the consultee in an organized manner. The consultant progressed in a smooth and logically concise fashion from the specification of general objectives to the designation of subordinate objectives and subsequently to the selection of a performance objective to be the immediate focus of consultation. One result of the consultant's highly organized approach was that he was able to conduct the interview quickly. Although this example was a developmental interview that involved the specification of a number of objectives, the conversation lasted about 10 minutes. One of the major points illustrated by this interview is that consultants can provide long-term developmental consultation for children without making excessive interview time demands on consultees.

Problem-Centered Consultation

The second case to be presented illustrates the use of problem-centered consultation to increase the number of times during each school day that a preschool boy talked to his teacher and to other adult socializing agents in the school setting. The initial plan, which was unsuccessful, involved the use of positive reinforcement, in the form of teacher attention, to increase the child's verbal behavior. A second plan, which used cuing, reinforcement, and extinction, was effective in increasing the child's talking.

The Problem Identification Interview

Consultant: (1) Who's the child who is of concern to you?

Consultee: His name is Walter. He's been coming to our school for about two years.

Consultant: (2) And what concerns you about Walter?

Consultee: Ah, he seems to be rather shy. He doesn't talk a lot.

Consultant: (3) Uh-huh, what does he do that shows you that he's shy?

Consultee: Well, when he comes in the morning, and we all say hello to him, he seems shy and won't say hello back. Things like that.

Consultant: (4) What other things show you that he's shy?

Consultee: Well, if he wants his shoe tied, he seems to be reluctant to ask us to tie his shoes, so he'll do something like just put his foot out, you know, for us to tie his shoe, and he won't ask for his shoe to be tied. Things like that. Or if we're having some kind of a project or we're working on something at a table, and other kids will be talking to us about what they're doing—"Teacher look at what I did," things like that. He doesn't do that. He'll just sit there, and he won't ask us to look at what he's done, or anything like that.

Consultant: (5) Then what concerns you is that Walter doesn't talk to you?

Consultee: Yes, right.

Consultant: (6) Are there any other things you mean when you say he's shy?

Consultee: I don't think so. I think that it's just that he won't talk to us when we talk to him or ask him questions. And then, he won't ask for things like materials that he needs. He'll just point or something like that.

Consultant: (7) Okay. Does he talk to other kids? (8) Does he talk to adults?

Consultee: Yes. He does talk to kids some.

Consultant: (9) So you're concerned that Walter doesn't talk to you. (10) And he doesn't talk to you when you ask him questions.

Consultee: Uh-huh, he doesn't talk to any of the teachers.

Consultant: (11) Okay, and he doesn't talk, for example, in group time when other kids . . . (12) he doesn't show you his work.

Consultee: Uh-huh.

Consultant: (13) Talk and show you his work.

Consultee: Right.

Consultant: (14) And he doesn't ask for things.

Consultee: Right.

Consultant: (15) Okay, how often would you say he does talk to you?

Consultee: It's hard to say. Very little, almost never.

Consultant: (16) How often did he talk to you today?

Consultee: I don't think that he talked to me at all today.

Consultant: (17) How often would you say in a week he does talk to you?

Consultee: Oh, maybe a few times, maybe a couple times, not more than that. Maybe a couple times a week.

Consultant: (18) So he's only talking to you a couple of times a week.

Consultee: Yes.

Consultant: (19) What is it, could you describe for me when it is that you expect him to talk, or you would expect him to talk and he doesn't talk?

Consultee: Ah, well, as I said, when he comes in the morning, or when we talk to him and he doesn't talk back.

Consultant: (20) Uh-huh.

Consultee: Ah, when the teachers just make comments to him, he doesn't talk back, or when we ask him questions—for instance, in group time—and the other kids will be talking and answering questions, but Walter doesn't want to answer questions. And as I said, he doesn't ask for materials.

Consultant: (21) What do you do when he doesn't talk or when he doesn't ask for materials?

Consultee: When he doesn't ask for materials, I guess what we do is go ahead and give him what he needs, you know, what he is pointing to. For a while, we did try ignoring his pointing to materials, but most of the time, I guess we go ahead and tie his shoe or give him the scissors that he needs, or whatever.

Consultant: (22) Okay, what do you do when you, say, ask him a question in the group, and he doesn't answer it?

Consultee: Ah, let me see. I sometimes ask the question more than once. I might ask him again or ask it in a different way or something like that.

Consultant: (23) Uh-huh.

Consultee: But when he doesn't say anything usually, I guess, I would go on to something or maybe ask another child to answer the question. If he can go ahead and do whatever I'm asking without talking, then that's fine. He does that, and then we go in.

Consultant: So Walter's not talking when he wants material. (25) Rather, he points. (1) In the group, when you ask him questions, he doesn't talk. (2) And then just as you said, he doesn't just spontaneously talk to you.

Consultee: Uh-huh.

Consultant: (3) And when you ask him something—when there's a situation when, for instance, maybe he should talk and he doesn't—you either give him what he wants or you just go on to someone else.

Consultee: Uh-huh.

Consultant: (4) The first thing we need to do is to get some baseline data. (5) We need to record Walter's behavior. (6) Do you know what baseline data are?

Consultee: Yes.

Consultant: (7) Okay, good. (8) It will be helpful to get some baseline data so that we know exactly what's happening. (9) And it will also help us evaluate whether the plan that we figure out next time will work.

Consultee: Yes.

Consultant: (10) You are basically concerned with how often Walter talks, (11) is that right?

Consultee: Yes.

Consultant: (12) Could you count how often Walter talks?

Consultee: Sure.

Consultant: (13) Okay, good. (14) You can do that by writing down a mark on a piece of paper whenever he talks to you.

Consultee: So just count whenever he does talk?

Consultant: (15) Right.

Consultee: Write that down?

Consultant: (16) Something else that would be really useful is if you could count how often some normal child—I mean, some child who talks as often as you would like Walter to talk—how often that child talks to you. (17) Is there some child who—say, if Walter talked as often as that child, you'd be happy?

Consultee: Well, Walter does play with a little boy he does talk to some, named Dewey. I could count how many times Dewey talks.

Consultant: (18) That'd be real helpful.

Consultee: Yes, because Dewey does talk to us and so . . .

Consultant: (19) So you're going to count how often Walter talks to you.

Consultee: Uh-huh.

Consultant: (20) And how often Dewey talks to you.

Consultee: Uh-huh.

Consultant: (21) Do you know how to graph?

Consultee: Uh-huh, we've done that.

Consultant: (22) Could you graph the data? (23) For instance, every day could you graph how often Walter talks to you and how often Dewey talks to you?

Consultee: Okay, I could do that.

Consultant: (24) Okay, great. (25) Now what time of the day could you do this recording?

Consultee: I don't know what you mean.

Consultant: (1) I mean, could you do it, do you want to do it all day?

Consultee: Oh, well I couldn't do it all day because they're not both there all day. I could do it in the mornings when they're both there.

Consultant: (2) That'd be really good.

Consultee: Okay, so when I graph it, I'll put each day and how many times each of them talked.

Consultant: (3) Right.

Consultee: Something like that?

Consultant: (4) Right. (5) Can I call you sometime next week and see how this data collection is going?

Consultee: Sure.

Consultant: (6) Well, let me call you on Tuesday or Wednesday.

Consultee: Fine.

Consultant: (7) So probably Tuesday or Wednesday when I call we can set up another meeting.

Consultee: That will be fine.

Consultant: (8) Okay, great.

Discussion of the Interview Transcript

The consultant's verbal behavior for the transcript of the problem identification interview presented above has been coded on consultation analysis record forms and is shown in Figure 2.4. The data in the figure indicate that the consultant was effective in her use of the content, process, and control message-classification categories. As should be the case, the bulk of the interview content fell in the behavior, the behavior-setting, and the observation subcategories. Moreover, the consultant maintained a high degree of focus in discussing various topics. Most of the utterances in the initial part of the interview were in the behavior subcategory. Then, the consultant shifted the focus of discussion to the behavior-setting classification. During the later stages of the interview, most of the utterances fell in the observation category.

The effectiveness of the consultant's interviewing skills is revealed in the use of the process category. As is appropriate, her utterances were generally restricted to the specification, summarization, and validation subcategories. The use of the control category in the interview was also effective. There were a large number of elicitors. Moreover, the use of emitters was restricted mainly to rendering summaries and to specifying recording procedures.

It may be instructive to look at some of the specific statements made by the consultant that were effective. Early in the interview, the consultant asked the consultee what it was about Walter's behavior that concerned her. The consultee responded that Walter was rather shy. Then, the consultant said, "What does he do that shows you that he's shy?" This question and other similar elicitors that followed re-

CONSULTATION-ANALYSIS RECORD

	Message Source		Message Content							Message Process							Message Control	
	Consultee	Consultant	Background Environment	Behavior Setting	Behavior	Individual Characteristics	Observation	Plan	Other	Negative Evaluation	Positive Evaluation	Inference	Specification	Summarization	Negative Validation	Positive Validation	Elicitor	Emitter
1	/								/				/				/	
2	/				/								/				/	
3	/			/									/				/	
4	/			/									/				/	
5	/			/										/				/
6	/			/												/	/	
7	/			/												/	/	
8	/			/												/	/	
9	/			/										/				/
10	/			/										/				/
11	/			/										/				/
12	/			/										/				/
13	/			/										/				/
14	/			/										/				/
15	/			/									/				/	
16	/			/									/				/	
17	/			/									/				/	
18	/			/										/				/
19	/		/											/			/	
20	/		/													/		/
21	/		/										/				/	
22	/		/										/				/	
23	/		/													/		/
24	/		/											/				/
25	/				/									/				/

FIGURE 2.4. Message classification analysis of consultant verbalizations in a problem-centered problem-identification interview.

CONSULTATION-ANALYSIS RECORD

	Message Source		Message Content							Message Process							Message Control	
	Consultee	Consultant	Background Environment	Behavior Setting	Behavior	Individual Characteristics	Observation	Plan	Other	Negative Evaluation	Positive Evaluation	Inference	Specification	Summarization	Negative Validation	Positive Validation	Elicitor	Emitter
1		/		/										/				/
2		/			/									/				/
3		/		/										/				/
4		/					/						/				/	
5		/					/						/				/	
6		/							/							/	/	
7		/							/			/						/
8		/					/					/						/
9		/					/					/						/
10		/			/									/				/
11		/			/											/	/	
12		/					/									/	/	
13		/					/					/						/
14		/					/						/					/
15		/					/									/		/
16		/					/					/						/
17		/							/							/	/	
18		/					/					/						/
19		/					/							/				/
20		/					/							/				/
21		/							/							/	/	
22		/					/						/				/	
23		/					/							/			/	
24		/					/						/					/
25							/							/			/	

Figure 2.4. (continued)

CONSULTANT Susan   CASE NUMBER 2

CONSULTEE Jane   INTERVIEW TYPE PII

                                                     PAGE 3

CONSULTATION-ANALYSIS RECORD

	Message Source		Message Content							Message Process							Message Control	
	Consultee	Consultant	Background Environment	Behavior Setting	Behavior	Individual Characteristics	Observation	Plan	Other	Negative Evaluation	Positive Evaluation	Inference	Specification	Summarization	Negative Validation	Positive Validation	Elicitor	Emitter
1		/					/									/	/	
2		/					/				/							/
3		/					/									/		/
4		/					/									/		/
5		/							/							/	/	
6		/							/				/					/
7		/							/			/						/
8		/							/		/							/
9																		
10																		
11																		
12																		
13																		
14																		
15																		
16																		
17																		
18																		
19																		
20																		
21																		
22																		
23																		
24																		
25																		

FIGURE 2.4. (*continued*)

vealed that what the consultee really meant by the term *shy* was that Walter did not converse with adults in the school environment. If the series of behavior specification elicitors that the consultant emitted early in the interview had not occurred, the problem might never have been defined in behavioral terms.

The failure to obtain a behavioral description of a subordinate goal was illustrated in the developmental interview discussed above. The following excerpt illustrates the consequences of lack of behavioral specificity in a case involving problem-centered consultation:

Consultant: Tell me about Jeffrey.

Consultee: Jeffrey started school in January, so it took him a while to get used to it and to the kids and the routine. He's pretty much used to that right now, but he still has a pretty big problem on the rug. He has an extremely difficult time focusing his attention, particularly when there are a lot of other children around. He tends to be a follower. If someone else is doing something, he feels he needs to do it in order to be in, to be accepted. He'll follow whatever they're doing. So, to me at least, right now, the biggest problem is his focusing attention on the rug when there are a lot of children around. He is pretty good at listening and responding individually, but it's when there's a group of four or more or especially the whole group together.

Consultant: The behavior you would like to zero in on then is paying attention?

Consultee: Yes.

Consultant: What generally happens before Jeffrey isn't paying attention?

The consultant in this brief interview excerpt accepted the consultee's vague description of Jeffrey's behavior, consequently, he or she did not obtain a precise specification of the problem that concerned the consultee. As a result, he or she could not determine the conditions surrounding the behavior and could not be certain what the consultee was recording when the data were collected.

Now consider Walter's case. After eliciting a behavioral description of Walter's shyness from the teacher, the consultant was in an excellent position to explore the conditions surrounding Walter's behavior. Her handling of the specification of antecedent conditions was particularly effective. Recall that the teacher described Walter's problem by focusing on his apparent reluctance to talk. Obviously, it would not have made sense for the consultant to attempt to establish the antecedents of not talking by saying "What generally happens right before Walter doesn't talk?" She understood this point yet was also aware that antecedent conditions could be important to the case. The consultant recognized that an implicit aspect of the teacher's complaint regarding Walter's "no-talking" behavior was an assumption that Walter should respond verbally to certain environmental cues. To determine the nature of those cues, the consultant asked, "When is it, could you describe for me when it is that you expect him to talk, or you would expect him to talk and he doesn't talk?" As will be discussed later, the consultant could have used the information that was obtained from this question during problem analysis in the design of a plan to increase talking. (Ironically, after recognizing the importance of the question, she failed to follow up on it during problem analysis, which is very likely one reason that the initial plan failed to achieve the desired results.)

The decision to ask the consultee when Walter was expected to talk served two purposes. It produced useful information regarding the available cues and signaled the need to verbalize, and it also established the consequences that followed the "not-talking behavior." Having identified the particular situations in which talking was expected to occur, the consultant was able to ask the teacher what she did following Walter's failure to speak in those situations. The information obtained in response to the consultant's query regarding the consequences of Walter's failure to speak was quite revealing. Recall that the teacher indicated that, when Walter failed to request materials verbally or refused to ask the teacher in words to tie his shoe, she generally attempted to respond to his needs by attending to his nonverbal cues. The teacher's comments about her reactions to Walter's nonverbal reactions suggest that he may have experienced positive reinforcement for nonverbal communication, which served as a substitute for verbal behavior.

During the discussion of recording procedures, the consultant made a decision that potentially had a marked effect on subsequent phases in the case. The teacher had indicated that Walter's problem was not talking. However, in the discussion of recording procedures, the consultant shifted the focus of conversation from Walter's failure to speak to a discussion of how to assess the number of times that he actually did speak. In this connection, the consultant said, "You're basically concerned with how often Walter talks, is that right?" After receiving an affirmative response to this question, the consultant went on to say, "Okay, could you count how often Walter talks?"

Two beneficial consequences followed the decision to record talking rather than lack of talking. First of all, talking was a very low-rate behavior for Walter. As a result, it was easy for the teacher to record it. Second, recording Walter's verbalizations refocused the evaluation on a positive accomplishment (the acceleration of Walter's verbal behavior), rather than on the elimination of something negative (Walter's failure to speak). Despite these advantages, one very unfortunate outcome was associated with the recording plan adopted. It provided no information that could be used to establish the conditions surrounding Walter's failure to speak. For example, the data provided no occasion for the consultant to ask the teacher what she did when Walter was expected to speak and did not. There was no record of the times when Walter ought to have spoken but did not do so. As a result, as will be discussed later in this guidebook, the consequences of Walter's failure to talk in situations when he was expected to speak were not discussed.

The consultant could have solved the recording problem by tabulating the percentage of occasions during each school day when Walter talked when he was expected to. This measure would have provided a record of positive accomplishment and would concurrently have presented data that might have stimulated a discussion of the events surrounding Walter's failure to communicate verbally. For example, the consultant might have asked the teacher to make a note of the situations in which Walter failed to respond verbally and of her reactions to Walter's lack of speech.

APPENDIX A
Reading Quiz

1. Problem identification plays a particularly important role in consultation because _____ _____.

2. The problem to be solved in consultation is _____ _____ _____.

3. The steps in problem identification are

   a. _____.

   b. _____.

   c. _____.

   d. _____.

   e. _____.

4. Objectives vary widely in specificity. The three levels of objectives are

   a. _____.

   b. _____.

   c. _____.

5. _____ is the most significant function of the general objectives.

6. The three defining characteristics of a performance objective are

   a. _____.

   b. _____.

   c. _____.

7. Providing _____ is one important function of the performance objective.

8. Two variations in approach to the problem-solving process are

   a. _____.

   b. _____.

9. _____
   consultation requires the establishment of general, subordinate, and performance objectives.

10. One advantage of behavioral observations is that _____

    _____.

11. Five questions that must be answered with regard to data collection are

    a. _____.

    b. _____.

    c. _____.

    d. _____.

    e. _____.

12. The amount of response is known as _____

    _____ .

13. _____ involve how many
    times a behavior occurs.

14. Recording during specified time intervals that are samples of the

    total recording time is known as _____ .

15. Continuous recording provides a very _____
    record of behavior.

16. The period of collecting baseline data can be quite short when (circle one)
    a. behavior is very unstable.
    b. behavior is highly stable.
    c. behavior occurs at a very low rate.

17. The _____ is usually responsible for collecting
    data.

18. In the problem identification interview, the consultant guides the consultee toward

    a. _____ .

    b. _____ .

19. In problem-centered consultation, the first goal-specification objective is _____ .

20. During the problem identification interview, an approximate specification of the incidence of the problem behavior is helpful because _____

    _____

    _____ .

21. The problem identification interview scripts provided as examples in this chapter demonstrate (circle one)
    a. problem-centered consultation.
    b. developmental consultation.
    c. both developmental consultation and problem-centered consultation.

22. In behavioral consultation, the consultant _____ ____ the kind of information that is obtained.

23. The consultant must help the consultee to translate vague, everyday speech into _____

    _____ .

24. Behavior must be specified precisely to

    a. _____ .

    b. _____ .

    c. _____ .

APPENDIX B

Reading Quiz Answers

1. When problem identification goes well, there is a good chance that a plan will be implemented.
2. Eliminating the discrepancy between existing client performance and desired performance.
3. a. establish objectives.
   b. establish measures.
   c. establish and implement data collection.
   d. display data.
   e. establish the discrepancy between current and desired client performance.
4. a. general.
   b. subordinate.
   c. performance.
5. Providing an organizational framework
6. a. a behavioral description of the desired activity.
   b. specification of performance conditions.
   c. precise indication of required performance level.
7. focus
8. a. developmental consultation.
   b. problem-centered consultation.
9. Developmental
10. it is possible to relate them to the objectives formulated.
11. a. What to record.
    b. how to record.
    c. when to record.
    d. How many observations.
    e. Who shall record.
12. magnitude of behavior.
13. Frequency data
14. sampling or time sampling.
15. complete
16. behavior is highly stable.
17. consultee
18. a. specification of objectives.
    b. designation of measurement procedures to be used.

19. to get a precise description of the behavior(s) of concern to the consultee.
20. it gives the consultant a rough indication of the problem's severity.
21. both developmental consultation and problem-centered consultation.
22. controls
23. behavioral definitions, objective terms, or objective language.
24. a. ensure its objective measurement.
    b. ensure clear communication between consultant and consultee.
    c. make it possible to investigate environmental influences on behavior.

Appendix C
Operational Definition Exercise

The following material is designed to provide some exercises for the consultant to help translate vague and general statements from a consultee into more specific and operational terminology. The individual studying this guidebook is requested to practice writing some specific behaviors that may be a part of a hypothetical, but realistic, statement from a consultee or client. *Consultee statement:* "My husband is very negative with the children."

List some possible behaviors that may make up or be related to this problem. Attempt to use the criteria for a good operational definition discussed in the chapter.

_____

_____

_____

_____

_____

Consultee statement: "The children are always getting into trouble and are driving me crazy."

_____

_____

_____

_____

_____

Consultee statement: "My child is completely out of control."

_____

_____

_____

_____

_____

Consultee statement: "John has a very poor self-concept."

_____

_____

_____

_____

_____

Consultee statement: "I always try to be firm with the children, but this doesn't appear to be working."

_____

_____

_____

_____

_____

APPENDIX D

Discussion Questions

The following questions are designed to elicit further considerations in problem identification and to promote discussion in group training sessions following viewing a problem identification videotape or a live example.

1. What importance do relationship variables play during the initial phases of consultation?
2. What are some limitations of concrete and specific target-behavior identification? What can be done about these limitations?
3. What are some examples of target behaviors that are difficult to operationalize during problem identification?
4. What are some barriers to the consultee's role in data collection?
5. What are some assessment methods and strategies that can be used by the consultant and/or the client to supplement consultee data-gathering?

APPENDIX E
Problem Identification Interview

Client's name: _____ Sex: _____

Address: _____

_____

School: _____ Grade: _____

Consultant: _____

Consultee: _____

	Year	Month	Day
Date of assessment:	_____	_____	_____
Birthdate:	_____	_____	_____
Age:	_____	_____	_____

Problem Identification Interview (PII)

Consultant note: The purposes of the PII are to

- Define the problem(s) in behavioral terms.

- Provide a tentative identification of behavior in terms of ante-cedent, situation, and consequent conditions.

- Provide a tentative strength of the behavior (e.g., how often or severe).

- Establish a procedure for the collection of baseline data in terms of the sampling plan and what behavior is to be recorded, who is to record it, and how it is to be recorded.

The consultant should question and/or comment in the following areas:
1. Opening salutation
2. General statement to introduce discussion (e.g., "Describe Diane's hyperactive behavior," or "Let's see, you referred Johnny because of his poor self-concept, lack of progress, and rebellious behavior. Which of these do you want to start with? Describe Johnny's rebellion (poor self-concept or lack of progress in the classroom)."

Record responses: _____

_____

_____

_____

_____

_____

3. Behavior specification (e.g., "What does Charles do when he is hyperactive?" or "What does Mary do when she is disrespectful?" A precise description of the behavior of concern to the consultee or client, e.g., "What does _____ do?")

   a. Specify examples: _____

_____

_____

_____

_____

_____

Important: Ask for as many examples of the problem behavior as possible.

b. Specify priorities: _____

_____

_____

_____

_____

Important: After eliciting all the examples that the consultee or client can give, ask which behavior is causing the most difficulty and establish a priority.

(*Note:* To help prioritize problems, ask the consultee or client, "On a scale of 0 to 10, where 0 = no problem and 10 = severe problem, how severe is the problem for you?")

4. Behavior setting (a precise description of the settings in which the problem behaviors occur, e.g., "Where does _____ do this?")

a. Specify examples (e.g., home, where in home): _____

_____

_____

_____

_____

_____

Important: Ask for as many examples of settings as possible.

b. Specify priorities: _____

_____

_____

_____

_____

_____

Important: After eliciting all the examples that the consultee or client can give, ask which setting is causing the most difficulty and establish priorities.

(*Note:* Settings may be ranked in the same manner as behaviors.)

5. Identify antecedents: What happens right before the problem behavior occurs? (e.g., "What happens before Mary makes an obscene gesture to the rest of the class?" or "What happens before George begins to hit other children?")

Record responses: _____

_____

_____

_____

_____

_____

6. Sequential conditions analysis: When during the day does the behavior occur and/or what is the pattern of antecedent–consequent conditions across several occurrences of the problem behavior (e.g., "When does Mary . . . ? Who is Mary with . . . ? What is Mary supposed to be doing when . . . ?")?

Record responses: _____

_____

_____

_____

_____

_____

7. Identify consequent conditions: What happens after the problem behavior has occurred? (e.g., "What happens after Mary . . . ?" or "What do the other students do when Charles climbs on the radiator?" or "What do you do when George hits other children?")

Record responses: _____

_____

_____

_____

_____

_____

8. Summarize and validate antecedent, consequent, and sequential conditions (e.g., "You've said that you and Timmy argue after you have asked him to do something, and he has refused. The argument continues as long as you try to talk to him. Is that correct?" or "You've said that at bedtime you tell Ava that it is time for bed, and that she doesn't answer you. You tell her again, and she says, 'Oh, Mom.' You remind her a third time, and she asks for 10 more minutes. You get mad, threaten to tell her father, and take her physically down to her room. She leaves her room approximately twice, asks for a drink of water, and finally falls asleep. Is that how it goes?")

Record responses: _____

_____

_____

_____

_____

_____

9. Behavior strength
   a. *Frequency:* How often a behavior occurs (e.g., "How often does Kevin have tantrums?").
   b. *Duration:* Length of time that a behavior occurs (e.g., "How long do Craig's tantrums last?").

Record responses: _____

_____

_____

_____

_____

_____

10. Summarize and validate behavior and behavior strength:
    a. "You have said that Jason makes you angry and upset by wet-
       ting his bed."
    b. "That he wets his bed approximately four times a week."
    c. "Is that right?"

Record responses: _____

_____

_____

_____

_____

_____

11. Tentative definition of goal—question consultee (e.g., "How
    often would Patrick have to turn in his work to get along okay?"
    or "How frequently could Charles leave his seat without causing
    problems?")

Record responses: _____

_____

_____

_____

_____

_____

12. Assets question: Determine what the student is good at (e.g., "Is
    there something that Mary does well?").

Record responses: _____

_____

_____

_____

_____

_____

13. Question about approach to teaching or existing procedures (e.g., "How long are Charles and the other students doing seat work problems?" or "What kind of . . . ?")

Record responses: _____

_____

_____

_____

_____

_____

14. Summarization statement and validation (e.g., "Let's see, the main problem is that Charles gets out of his seat and runs around the room during independent work assignments. He does this about four times each day. Is that right?")

Record responses: _____

_____

_____

_____

_____

_____

15. Directional statement to provide rationale for data recording (e.g., "We need some record of Sarah's completion of homework assignments, how often assignments are completed, what assignments are completed, and so on. This record will help us to deter-

mine how frequently the behavior is occurring, and it may give us some clues to the nature of the problem. Also, the record will help us decide whether any plan we initiate has been effective.")

Record responses: _____

_____

_____

_____

_____

16. Discuss data collection procedures. Data may be collected in four ways:
   a. *Real-time recording*
      Advantages:
      —Provides unbiased estimates of frequency and duration.
      —Data are capable of complex analyses such as conditional probability analysis.
      —Data are susceptible to sophisticated reliability analysis.
      Disadvantages:
      —Demanding task for observers.
      —May require costly equipment.
      —Requires that responses have clearly distinguishable beginnings and ends.
   b. *Event or duration recording*
      Advantages:
      —Measures are of a fundamental response characteristic (i.e., frequency or duration).
      —Can be used by participant-observers (e.g., parents or teachers) with low rate responses.
      Disadvantages:
      —Requires responses to have clearly distinguishable beginnings and ends.
      —Unless responses are located in real time (e.g., by dividing a session into brief recording intervals), some forms of reliability assessment may be impossible.

—May be difficult with multiple behaviors unless mechanical aids are available.

c. *Momentary time samples*
Advantages:
—Response duration of primary interest.
—Time saving and convenient.
—Useful with multiple behaviors and/or children.
—Applicable to responses without clear beginnings or ends.
Disadvantages:
—Unless samples are taken frequently, continuity of behavior may be lost.
—May miss most occurrences of brief, rare responses.

d. *Interval recording*
Advantages:
—Sensitive to both response frequency and response duration.
—Applicable to a wide range of responses.
—Facilitates observer training and reliability assessments.
—Applicable to responses without clearly distinguishable beginnings and ends.
Disadvantages:
—Confounds frequency and duration.
—May under- or overestimate response frequency and duration.

Record responses: _____

_____

_____

_____

_____

_____

17. Summarize and validate recording procedures (e.g., "We have agreed that you will record the amount of time that Doug's tantrums last by recording the start and stop times. You will do this for 3 days and you will use this form. You will also record what happens before the behavior occurs and what you do after it has occurred. Is this okay with you?")

Record responses: _____

_____

_____

_____

_____

_____

18. Establish a date to begin data collection.

Record responses: _____

_____

_____

_____

_____

19. Establish date of next appointment.

    Record response: Date _____

                     Day _____

                     Time _____

                     Place _____

20. Closing salutation.

Problem Identification Interview Data Sheet

Date: _____ Observer: _____

Client: _____ Reliability: _____

Consultee: _____ Observer: _____

Consultant: _____ Session #: _____

Interview objective	Occurrence	Response
1. Opening salutation		
2. General statement		
3. Behavior specification		
a. Specify examples		
b. Specify priorities		
4. Behavior setting		
a. Specify examples		
b. Specify priorities		
5. Identify antecedents		
6. Identify sequential conditions		
7. Identify consequences		
8. Summarize and validate		
9. Behavior strength		
10. Summarize and validate		
11. Tentative definition of goal		
12. Assets question		
13. Question about existing procedures		

14. Summarize and validate   _____   _____

15. Directional statement about
    data recording   _____   _____

16. Data collection procedures   _____   _____

17. Summarize and validate   _____   _____

18. Date to begin data
    collection   _____   _____

19. Establish date of next
    appointment   _____   _____

20. Closing salutation   _____   _____

3

Problem Analysis

On completion of this chapter, the reader should be able to:

1. Name the five steps in problem analysis.
2. Name and describe three kinds of conditions that may affect behavior.
3. State the major functions of antecedent, consequent, and sequential conditions when the goal of consultation is to (a) increase, (b) decrease, or (c) maintain behavior.
4. State the steps in conducting a conditions analysis.
5. Compare and contrast plan strategies and plan tactics.
6. State the objectives of the problem analysis interview.

Introduction

Problem analysis is undertaken when the data collected during problem identification indicate the existence of a target problem(s). During problem analysis, the consultant and the consultee jointly identify factors that may lead to problem resolution. For example, the consultant may assist the consultee in focusing on variables such as the setting, intrapersonal child characteristics, or skill deficits of the child. The consultant and the consultee use the identified factors to develop a plan designed to achieve a solution to the client's problem(s).

The Problem Analysis Process

The problem analysis process includes the following steps: (1) choosing an analysis procedure; (2) conducting conditions and/or skills analysis; (3) developing plan strategies; (4) developing plan tactics; and (5) establishing procedures to assess performance during implementation. These steps occur in two broad phases. The first phase involves an analysis of factors that may lead to problem solution (i.e., the analysis phase). The second phase involves the development of a plan (or treatment) to solve the problem (i.e., the plan design phase).

111

THE ANALYSIS PHASE

General Considerations

There are two ways to identify factors that may influence the behavior of concern: (1) focus on conditions that could affect goal attainment, and (2) analyze the kinds of client skills necessary to achieve the goal. The first step in problem analysis is to decide whether to focus on the analysis of conditions or skills, or both. There are no hard-and-fast rules that one can invariable apply in making this decision. However, there are certain general guidelines that may be helpful in selecting an appropriate analysis procedure.

One of the purposes of consultation is to promote self-direction on the part of the client; thus, problem analysis should generally include a consideration of the skills necessary for the child to achieve self-direction. For example, suppose that the goals of consultation are to reduce a child's disruptive behavior and to assist the child to achieve an adequate level of control over his or her behavior. In this situation, it would be useful to inform the teacher of techniques that he or she can use to control the disruptive behavior and strategies that may help the child maintain self-control.

When the goal of consultation is to increase or to maintain the target behavior, and the information obtained during problem identification reveals variability in the level of behavior, problem analysis should generally focus on conditions that may influence behavior rather than on specific skill acquisition. For example, suppose that a boy is doing poorly in spelling. An examination of four or five samples of his written work and a standardized assessment reveal that his overall performance is inconsistent. In other words, at times he performs very well and on other occasions he does not do well. Insofar as the child can meet high performance standards on some occasions, it is reasonable to assume that he or she could meet them on most, if not all, occasions. Under these circumstances, the most likely variables to examine in an effort to attain problem solution are the conditions that influence spelling behavior.

Even if variability in performance is not evident, situational or environmental conditions may be factors that should be considered during problem analysis. Preliminary explorations during problem identification may reveal environmental circumstances that have a marked impact on the attainment of consultation goals. For example, suppose that, in the case of the child who is having spelling difficulties, poor work samples are often followed by extra attention from the child's parents. In these circumstances, potential influences of the environmental variables must be considered, even if the child's performance in spelling is uniformly inadequate.

When the goal of the consultation is to increase or to maintain behavior, the level of performance is uniformly low, and preliminary exploration suggests that the existing conditions generally support goal attainment, the principal focus of problem analysis should be on the identification of skills related to the attainment of specified goals. For example, if all of the children in a class were having difficulty in mastering multiplication, the consultant and the consultee might examine the extent to which the children had attained mastery over the prerequisite skills in areas such as counting, grouping, and addition (see Bergan & Kratochwill, 1990, for a more detailed discussion).

Analyzing Conditions of Client Behavior

The consultant's main task during conditions analysis is to identify the psychological and educational principles that are related to the conditions associated with the client's behavior and that can be used to achieve specific consultation goals. The consultant should select principles that are pertinent to a particular problem. After the consultant and the consultee discuss the relevant psychological and educational variables, the consultant can match the existing conditions with conditions that the professional literature and knowledge suggest will lead to goal attainment.

In most cases, there will be a large number of variables that could influence client behavior. Problem analysis should focus on all variables that influence the problem. Because the number of factors that can affect behavior is large, the consultant must develop a strategy for classifying conditions that potentially influence client behavior. One method is to analyze antecedent, consequent, and sequential conditions and the function they may serve in consultation (see the discussion in Chapter 2).

Recall from Chapter 2 that antecedent conditions occur before a behavior and that consequent conditions are events that occur immediately after behavior. Sequential conditions indicate the time of day or the day of the week when the behavior of concern occurs or the patterning of antecedent and/or consequent conditions across a series of occasions. Therefore, typical questions asked by the consultant during conditions analysis are: When does this happen? With whom and where? What happened then? And what did you do then? The potential function served in consultation by antecedent, consequent, and sequential conditions vary in relation to the actual goals of consultation.

When the goal of consultation is to increase behavior, antecedent conditions serve several distinct functions. First, antecedent conditions can be manipulated to enhance response capability. For example, children are often required to emit responses that have been modeled for them. However, in some instances, a response may be too complex for the child to perform. It may be helpful to reduce the complexity by breaking the response into its component parts. In teaching a severely handicapped child eating skills, the components of a task might be broken down into how to hold a fork, how to use it to pick up food, and where to put the fork when it is not needed (see Morris, 1985, for examples of various programs).

Second, antecedent conditions may be used as a source of information about the stimuli to which the child is trying to respond, as well as about the kind of response he or she is to make. For example, a child may not control his or her behavior appropriately because he or she does not recognize cues that tell when reinforcement may occur. The consultant can suggest the use of prompts and cues, such as giving a simple verbal instruction or a gesture, or actually taking the client through the sequence of performance to enhance behavior control.

When the goal of consultation is to increase or decrease behavior, consequent conditions may be manipulated. Table 3.1 provides a summary of the major behavior-analysis intervention strategies that may be used to analyze consequent conditions. The reader who desires a more detailed presentation of these strategies in applied settings should consult some major works in the area (e.g., Kazdin, 1989; Morris, 1985; Sulzer-Azaroff & Mayer, 1977). Of special importance in

TABLE 3.1.   Basic Behavior-Analysis Intervention Strategies

Principle	Procedure	Functional behavioral effect
Positive reinforcement	Presentation of a stimulus following a target behavior.	Increase in response frequency.
Negative reinforcement	Removal of a stimulus following a target behavior.	Increase in response frequency.
Punishment	Presentation of a stimulus following a target behavior.	Decrease in response frequency.
Time-out	Removal of a stimulus following a target behavior.	Decrease in response frequency.
Extinction	Discontinuation of a reinforcing stimulus following a target behavior.	Decrease in response frequency of previously reinforced behavior.
Stimulus control and discrimination training	Reinforcement of a target behavior in the presence of one stimulus (S^D) but not in the presence of another (S).	Increase in response frequency in the presence of the S^D and decrease in response frequency in the presence of the S.

the analysis of consequences is the powerful influence that reinforcement plays in the maintenance of behaviors. A positive reinforcer is defined as any event following a given response that increases the chances of that response's occurring again. Typical positive reinforcers are tangible items such as money or food, social events such as praise or attention, and activities such as the chance to play or to watch television. In general, positive reinforcement is used to develop and maintain a new behavior or a set of new behaviors. The removal of a specific event following the target behavior that results in increased frequency of response is called *negative reinforcement*.

Another procedure used to reduce or eliminate behavior is punishment. Punishment occurs when an aversive stimulus is presented immediately following a response, resulting in a reduction in the rate of the particular response. We believe that punishment is a procedure that should generally be avoided in behavioral consultation. In fact, there are a number of alternatives to punishment that can be used. The reader is referred to LaVigna and Donnellan (1986) for a comprehensive review of alternative positive procedures that can be used in applied settings. The consultant should avoid punishment procedures whenever possible because they may cause the client to view the consultee as an aversive figure. In addition, the effects of punishment could generalize to other responses that should be increased, not reduced. Punishment may also become a pleasant experience for the consultee and may be applied in inappropriate situations.

When absolutely necessary, punishment is one of two major consequent conditions that can reduce behavior strength. It can be applied either by withdrawing a positive reinforcer (often called *timeout*) or by adding an aversive stimulus. For example, a child may be punished for aggressive behaviors by being deprived of watching television or by a verbal reprimand for the undesirable behavior.

Another major consequent condition that can be used to reduce behavior strength is extinction. This procedure involves the withdrawal of a positive reinforcer that has previously maintained a behavior. Withdrawal of attention through ignoring is one example of a highly effective extinction procedure that may be useful in consultation. However, it has three characteristics that limit its usefulness. First, it generally requires that the consultee do nothing in an active way to alter behavior. Second, behavior on extinction often increases sharply before it begins to diminish. Third, it sometimes does not eliminate the behavior of concern quickly. These problems associated with extinction can be ameliorated by combining extinction with other procedures. For example, to reduce aggressive behavior, the parent may ignore aggression and at the same time reinforce an incompatible behavior such as cooperation.

Stimulus control procedures must also be considered in a consequent analysis. In some cases a response may be followed by a reinforcing or punishing consequence in the presence of one stimulus (S^D), but not in the presence of another (S). In short, a response reinforced in one situation, but not in another situation, is influenced by the different situations. Thus, a particular situation increases the probability that the response will occur when compared to a situation previously associated with no reinforcement. Stimulus control occurs when there are different responses to different stimuli. For example, a child may be reinforced for math assignment completion in the classroom, but not at home. In this case, different reinforcement contingencies are associated with each situation, and the child may exhibit contrasting behaviors in the two settings.

Altering sequential behaviors is often the method of choice when seeking to increase behavior. Shaping is the most common sequential condition used to increase or elicit new responses. Shaping involves the reinforcement of approximations of the desired behavior. The consultee selects an appropriate initial response, elicits the response, and immediately reinforces the correct behavior. This shaping procedure is applied successively until the final desirable behavior is reached. For example, the desired target behavior might be for a child to dress herself in the morning. It may be necessary to place her legs in her underpants and require her only to pull the pants up, and then give praise and a hug. The next step in shaping might involve putting one leg in the pants and requiring the child to insert the other leg before pulling up the pants and receiving reinforcement. When this step is accomplished, the requirement might be for the child to complete the entire procedure. The series of steps necessary to conduct a conditions analysis are:

1. Specify whether the goal is to increase, decrease, or maintain behavior.
2. Identify the antecedent, consequent, and sequential conditions associated with the behavior.
3. Determine the existing conditions that may affect the behavior by matching the existing conditions with conditions that research has indicated have the potential to influence behavior.
4. Identify conditions not currently associated with the behavior that nonetheless could affect the behavior.

Analyzing Client Skills

Sometimes, consultation indicates the need to analyze skills that the client does not possess and that therefore represent appropriate targets for instruction (e.g., social skills). Skills analysis involves specifying behaviors that are components of goal behaviors. These components should be stated as performance objectives, and the consultant should continue to break skills down in the manner until he or she is satisfied that the client possesses the level of capabilities identified.

THE PLAN DESIGN PHASE

The second major phase of problem analysis is plan design. During this phase the consultant and the consultee develop procedures to put into effect during the treatment implementation phase of consultation.

Developing Plan Strategies

The first step in designing a plan is to specify broad strategies that can be used to achieve the goals of consultation. Plan strategies indicate possible courses of action that may be implemented in general terms. They provide ways to introduce psychological and educational principles based on prior research into the problem-solving process. The plan strategies used should be formulated directly as a result of the conditions and skills analyses that were conducted during the problem analysis phase. This formulation facilitates the consultant's application of general principles to the specific problems.

Developing Plan Tactics

After the plan strategy has been designated, plan tactics are used to implement the strategy. In essence, the plan strategy provides the principle to be applied, and the tactics provide a way to implement the principle. Plan tactics should include a description of the procedures and materials to be used. For example, if positive reinforcement were to be used, it would be necessary to establish the specific kinds of reinforcers and how they would be delivered. In addition, plan tactics should include a specification of the person responsible for carrying out the plan tactic, as well as the conditions for when the tactics will occur.

During the process of translating principles into practice, constraints operating in the client's environment may affect the kinds of tactics that can be applied. Practical factors such as time, expenses, and personnel must be considered. In addition to practical limitations, constraints associated with attitudes and values of the client should also be considered. This process involves an assessment of the treatment's acceptability to the consultee and the client (see next section).

Preimplementation Treatment Acceptability

The behavioral consultant should assess whether the treatment is appropriate and whether it accomplishes socially important goals. There is growing interest in assessment of the social validity and acceptability of behavioral treatments (see Witt & Elliott, 1985, for a review of this literature). There are two major reasons for assessment of the acceptability of treatments. First, legal and ethical concerns are posed by some interventions. Obtaining consumer input (from the teacher/or parent and the child) increases the number of factors that may be considered within an ethical context. Second, assessment of the acceptability of treatments may increase the likelihood that they will be used and implemented with integrity and that they will prove beneficial to consumers.

A number of scales have been used to assess the acceptability of treatments. The major ones that have been used in research include the Treatment Evaluation Inventory (Kazdin, 1980), the Intervention Rating Profile (IRP; Witt & Martens, 1983), and the Children's Intervention Rating Profile (CIRP; Elliott, 1986). We recommend using the brief version of the IRP-15 (Martens, Witt, Elliott, & Darveaux, 1985) and the CIRP. Although both devices are still in the experimental phase, some data on their respective psychometric properties are available (see Witt & Elliott, 1985, for a review). Both instruments are presented in Appendix E.

Establishing Performance Assessment Objectives

The final step in plan design is to establish performance assessment procedures to be used during plan implementation. When the plan to be implemented is based on conditions analysis, the specification of assessment procedures requires reaffirming the baseline procedures established during problem identification.

If plan implementation involves skill development, the problem of establishing assessment procedures requires provisions for collecting data on performance related to the terminal objectives to be achieved through consultation. In addition, plans for obtaining data on the acquisition of skills leading to the attainment of terminal objectives must be developed. Assessment procedures established for prerequisite skills should focus on the point at which each of the various skills is mastered.

THE PROBLEM ANALYSIS INTERVIEW

The process of analyzing the problem is initiated in the problem analysis interview. In this interview, the consultant and the consultee decide on the existence of a problem that warrants problem analysis. If they agree that there is a problem, conditions and/or skills that may influence the client's behavior are discussed. The consultee and the consultant then design a plan for achieving a solution to the problem. Problem analysis objectives include validating the problem, analyzing the problem and related variables, designing a plan, and developing procedural goals.

Problem Validation Objectives

The initial task to be accomplished during the problem analysis interview is to validate the existence of a problem. In some cases, baseline data may reveal that the problem is not as serious as first thought. In this case, consultation is either terminated or a new problem is identified.

The consultant's first objective is to determine the adequacy of the baseline data collected during problem identification. The consultant should examine the baseline data collected by the consultee and then plot or graph the data to provide a visual picture. An examination of the data should provide some insight into the problem.

The consultant's second objective with respect to problem valida-tion is to determine whether a discrepancy exists between the client's present performance and the desired performance. This determina-tion is accomplished by comparing the baseline level of performance with the goal established with respect to performance. When perfor-mance levels have not been established before the problem analysis interview (as is often the case in problem-centered consultation), the level is specified at this time.

The consultant's final objective with respect to problem valida-tion is to establish agreement between himself or herself and the consultee regarding the existence of a problem.

Analysis Objectives

In cases involving conditions analysis, the consultant's primary task is to determine conditions that may influence the client's attain-ment of the goals of consultation. This process includes a specifica-tion of the conditions currently existing in the client's environment and conditions that, though not currently operating, may affect client behavior.

In those cases involving skills analysis, the consultant's main task is to communicate the results of his or her assessment of client skills to the consultee. A consultant's second objective in these cases is to obtain information about the techniques used to enhance the client's performance of the terminal objectives during baseline. The focus of the interview should be on discovering whether there have been any changes in the instructional procedures. The consultant should ask about antecedent, consequent, and sequential conditions that define the procedures that the consultee used during baseline to enhance client performance.

Plan-Design Objectives

The first plan-design objective is to establish plan strategies that may be used in treatment implementation. The consultant frequently assumes responsibility for suggesting these strategies, especially if the consultee lacks information about and knowledge of the possible strategies. The consultant should provide strategies when the consultee requests specific information regarding ways to resolve the problem.

Although the consultant often finds it necessary to suggest the strategies to be used in the plan design, there are also distinct advantages in eliciting the strategies from the consultee. One advantage is that the consultee may be more likely to undertake and support strategies that he or she has helped to devise. It is unlikely that the consultee would suggest a strategy that he or she would not consider using. Regardless of who devises the strategies, the consultee makes the final decision concerning which strategies will be used in the treatment. The consultant's task is to find both workable and acceptable strategies and to facilitate collaborative efforts by both parties.

The second plan-design objective is to establish treatment plan tactics. It is usually a good idea to ask the consultee to indicate tactics that may be helpful in implementing strategies. The consultee has more knowledge of the client and can usually determine which tactic will be most effective. In addition, the consultee has knowledge of the constraints and resources in the client's environment.

The final plan-design objective is establishing performance assessment procedures to be used in treatment plan implementation. When the plan design is based on conditions analysis, the specification of assessment involves a continuation of the procedures established during baseline. However, when the plan design is based on skills analysis, the consultant and the consultee should agree on the types of measures to be used, the skills to be assessed, the number of data to be collected on each skill, when the data should be collected on each skill, and who should collect the data.

Procedural Objectives

The first procedural objective in problem analysis is setting a date for the problem evaluation interview. The date selected should be determined by the estimated length of time needed to achieve the goals. Generally, no more than a few weeks should elapse between the problem analysis and the treatment-plan evaluation interview. In those cases involving long-term goals, it is best to break the problem into specific goals that can be achieved quickly.

The second procedural objective during problem analysis is to make provisions to monitor the implementation process. The consultant should make arrangements to call or visit the consultee during the first few days of implementation. This follow-up allows the consultant to make sure the plan is being implemented properly and to make changes if necessary.

The final procedural objective involves consultee training. In some cases, the consultant may need to educate the consultee in the procedures to be used during implementation. The consultant must make arrangements concerning where and how training will occur. Again, a more detailed review of consultee training is found in Bergan and Kratochwill (1990).

Problem-Analysis-Interview Example

The Problem Analysis Interview

The following is an example of a problem-analysis interview:

Consultant: (1) Let's look at the data, (2) okay?

Consultee: Yes.

Consultant: (3) So Walter's spoken to you only twice in all this time.

Consultee: Uh-huh.

Consultant: (4) And Dewey's talking to you between 6 and about 10 times a day.

Consultee: Uh-huh.

Consultant: (5) So it really looks as if there's a problem.

Consultee: Yes, only twice, that's all.

Consultant: (6) What happened those two times when Walter did talk to you?

Consultee: One of them was when he wanted his shoe tied.

Consultant: (7) And what did he do? (8) Describe for me what happened.

Consultee: Well, he came up to me . . . I was just sitting at the table. He started to put his foot out to have it tied, his shoe tied, and he said something like "shoe." And I was real pleased to hear that, and I tied his shoe, of course. But it was really soft. You know, he still seemed shy, but he did say something, he said, "Shoe."

Consultant: (9) What about the other time?

Consultee: The other time was when, after school was over. He was going home and I said, "Bye, Walter," and he did say, "Good-bye."

Consultant: (10) Let's take yesterday. (11) Dewey spoke to you six times. (12) Would you describe a couple of those?

Consultee: Well, when he came in the morning he said hello. He asked me when snack time was, I remember. You know, "Is it time for snacks yet?" or something like that. Let me think. I remember that he told me that he wanted to paint. He wanted to do some painting. I can't really think of any others right now.

Consultant: (13) Okay.

Consultee: I can't remember.

Consultant: (14) So Walter—in the last 3 weeks, Walter's talked only twice, and (15) those were when he wanted something and when you said something to him.

Consultee: Uh-huh.

Consultant: (16) Okay, and Dewey's talking to you. (17) He's asking you questions. And he's . . .

Consultee: Uh-huh, like when is snack time.

Consultant: (18) Asking for materials and . . .

Consultee: He said, "hi."

Consultant: (19) Right.

Consultee: And I can't remember what else he was saying yesterday.

Consultant: (20) What we need to do is to make up a plan, to see if we can't get Walter talking to you. Is there some kind of . . . (21) What does Walter like? (22) What does Walter like to do around school?

Consultee: Well, he doesn't play on the equipment a lot, so you don't see him playing on the equipment. He does like to play cowboys; it is what he likes to do. Yes, he does like to play cowboy, but not on the equipment.

Consultant: (23) Is there some way that you could attend to Walter, give Walter some attention if he did talk?

Consultee: Yes. I think if we paid too much attention to him, I think he would kind of draw back. You know, if we paid a lot of attention to him when he said something, I think he just might withdraw.

Consultant: (24) What would be likely to happen if Walter were playing cowboy and he said something to one of the other kids and you praised him for talking?

Consultee: Things like that have happened before, and usually, what he does usually is hide or turn away or something like that. I don't think that would be too good.

Consultant: (25) Okay.

Consultee: He just seems to be too shy when we pay too much attention to him is what it is. I think if we overload him with a lot of affection, I think he would just be too shy.

Consultant: (1) Is there some other way you could pay attention to him?

Consultee: Well, I could do things like seeing that his shoes are tied. He brings that up a lot. It seems like he wants to get attention by getting his shoes tied. So I could certainly do that kind of thing: check his shoes, see if he needs a Kleenex, or something like that; see that he has materials; something that's not real obvious, that wouldn't require a whole pouring on of attention. I could do something like that.

Consultant: (2) Could you do it when he talks to other children?

Consultee: Uh-huh. I don't see why not, sure.

Consultant: (3) Okay, well let's try that.

Consultee: Okay. I might not be able to catch all the times that he is talking.

Consultant: (4) Oh, sure.

Consultee: But when I see him, I could do that.

Consultant: (5) Okay, good. (6) So you are going to pay attention to Walter, like by checking his shoe . . .

Consultee: Uh-huh.

Consultant: . . . and checking things . . .

Consultee: Yes.

Consultant: (7) Right?

Consultee: Right.

Consultant: (8) Can you continue to collect that same kind of data that you've been collecting?

Consultee: Uh-huh. The same thing, when he's talking to me.

Consultant: (9) Right.

Consultee: Uh-huh, sure. I can keep doing that.

Consultant: (10) Okay. Well, let's try that and see if that works.

Consultee: Okay.

Consultant: (11) I'd like to call . . . What do you . . . (12) Thursday's Thanksgiving. (13) When do you have classes here?

Consultee: We do come back on Friday.

Consultant: (14) Well, I'm going out of town so I won't . . . (15) I mean, there's not a whole lot of point calling you tomorrow.

Consultee: Yes.

Consultant: (16) I won't be here Friday. (17) We could just get together next week and see how it's going.

Consultee: Okay.

Consultant: (18) When's good for you?

Consultee: How about Tuesday? Would that be good for you?

Consultant: (19) Okay, so we'll get together Tuesday. (20) Here, at 3 o'clock?

Consultee: Okay, that's fine.

Consultant: (21) And you're going to collect those same kind of data.

Consultee: Uh-huh, right. And pay attention with the shoes when he's talking.

Consultant: (22) Good.

Discussion of the Interview Transcript

The consultation-analysis record shown in Figure 3.1 reveals a major error in the conduct of the problem analysis interview. The number of statements in the behavior-setting subcategory is less than half the number of utterances in either the behavior or plan subcategories. As indicated earlier, the consultant should strive to make the number of utterances in these three classifications about equal during problem analysis.

The main consequence of slighting the behavior-setting subcategory in problem analysis is generally that the consultant and the consultee fail to consider the conditions currently associated with the client's behavior in constructing a plan to change the behavior. This failure is precisely what happened in Walter's case. The formulation of a plan to change Walter's behavior did not follow from an analysis of the conditions recognized as potential sources of influence on Walter's speaking. After signaling the need to make a plan, the consultant initiated conversation about that topic by asking what kind of things Walter liked to do around school. It became apparent shortly after this comment that her plan strategy was to introduce a new reinforcer or set of reinforcers into the situation in an effort to increase the frequency of Walter's verbalizations.

As pointed out above, it seems probable that the consultant's failure to consider the conditions currently associated with Walter's verbal behavior stemmed, at least in part, from the decision that she

CONSULTATION-ANALYSIS RECORD

	Message Source		Message Content							Message Process							Message Control	
	Consultee	Consultant	Background Environment	Behavior Setting	Behavior	Individual Characteristics	Observation	Plan	Other	Negative Evaluation	Positive Evaluation	Inference	Specification	Summarization	Negative Validation	Positive Validation	Elicitor	Emitter
1	/				/								/				/	
2	/				/											/	/	
3	/				/									/				/
4	/				/									/				/
5	/				/							/						/
6	/			/									/				/	
7	/				/								/				/	
8	/			/									/				/	
9	/			/									/				/	
10	/				/								/				/	
11	/				/								/					/
12	/				/								/				/	
13	/			/												/		/
14	/				/									/				/
15	/			/										/				/
16	/				/									/				/
17	/				/									/				/
18	/				/									/				/
19	/				/											/		/
20	/							/					/				/	
21	/				/								/				/	
22	/				/								/				/	
23	/							/								/	/	
24	/							/				/					/	
25	/							/								/		/

FIGURE 3.1. Message classification analysis of consultant verbalizations in a problem-centered problem-analysis interview.

CONSULTANT Susan   CASE NUMBER 2

CONSULTEE Jane   INTERVIEW TYPE PAI

                                            PAGE 2

CONSULTATION-ANALYSIS RECORD

	Message Source		Message Content							Message Process							Message Control	
	Consultee	Consultant	Background Environment	Behavior Setting	Behavior	Individual Characteristics	Observation	Plan	Other	Negative Evaluation	Positive Evaluation	Inference	Specification	Summarization	Negative Validation	Positive Validation	Elicitor	Emitter
1		/						/								/	/	
2		/						/								/	/	
3		/						/					/				/	
4		/						/								/		/
5		/						/			/							/
6		/						/						/				/
7		/						/								/	/	
8		/					/									/	/	
9		/					/									/		/
10		/						/					/				/	
11		/							/			/						/
12		/							/				/					/
13		/							/				/				/	
14		/							/				/					/
15		/							/	/								/
16		/							/				/					/
17		/							/				/					/
18		/							/				/				/	
19		/							/					/				/
20		/							/							/	/	
21		/					/							/				/
22		/					/					/						/
23																		
24																		
25																		

FIGURE 3.1. (*continued*)

made regarding the recording of behavior during problem identification. If the teacher had included information regarding the occasions on which Walter was expected to speak but did not, the discussion of the baseline data might have involved some specification of the kinds of situations in which Walter failed to verbalize and an indication of the teacher's precise behaviors in response to Walter's failure to speak. If information on these matters had been elicited, it might have been incorporated into the plan to change Walter's behavior.

Although the consultant failed to link conditions analysis to plan design, she was highly effective in eliciting plan tactics from the consultee. For example, at one point, the consultant said, "Is there some way that you could attend to Walter, give some attention to Walter if he did talk?" A few sentences later, the consultant remarked, "What would be likely to happen if Walter were playing cowboy and he said something to one of the other kids and you praised him for talking?"

The consultant's use of elicitors in establishing plan tactics served a useful purpose. It highlighted constraints and resources in the consultee's environment that might affect the plan design. For example, in response to the consultant's question regarding whether paying attention to Walter for speaking would be feasible, the consultee responded, "You know, if we paid a lot of attention to him when he said something, I think he just might withdraw." The consultant might not have been aware that the teacher had this reservation about the use of attention if she had simply told the teacher to use attention rather than asking for her views on the subject. Later in the conversation, the consultee indicated the kinds of reinforcers that, in her view, could be applied to increase Walter's speech. In this regard, she said, "Well, I could do things like seeing that his shoes are tied." It is interesting to note that the reinforcers that the teacher mentioned for use in the plan design fell in the same categories as those consequent conditions discussed during problem identification. As pointed out in the discussion of the problem identification interview, those conditions may have served as reinforcers for nonverbal substitutes for speech behaviors. It is particularly significant that the plan formulated in the problem analysis interview did nothing to preclude the possibility that those consequent conditions would continue to reinforce nonverbal communication patterns.

During the final stages of the problem analysis interview, an unfortunate circumstance arose that added to the difficulties involved in achieving a solution to Walter's problem. The consultant wanted to contact the teacher after the plan had been put into effect for a brief period. However, she was unable to do this. Consequently, even though the plan did not work, it remained in operation for an extended period of time.

APPENDIX A
Reading Quiz

1. Problem analysis is undertaken when _____

   _____

   _____ .

2. The two broad phases of problem analysis are

   a. _____ .

   b. _____ .

3. The steps in problem analysis are to

   a. _____ .

   b. _____ .

   c. _____ .

   d. _____ .

   e. _____ .

4. List and define three kinds of conditions that may affect behavior:

   _____

   _____

   _____

   _____

   _____

5. Compare and contrast plan strategies and plan tactics:

   _____

   _____

   _____

   _____

   _____

APPENDIX B

Reading Quiz Answers

1. The data collected during problem identification indicates the existence of a problem.
2. a. The analysis phase
   b. The plan design phase
3. a. Choose an analysis procedure
   b. Conduct a conditions analysis
   c. Develop plan strategies
   d. Develop plan tactics
   e. Establish procedures to assess performance during implementation
4. a. Antecedent—occurs just before a behavior
   b. Consequent—occurs just after a behavior
   c. Sequential—patterning of events across a series of occasions

5. *Plan strategies* indicate in general terms a possible course of action that can be taken during the treatment-plan-implementation phase of consultation. They are devised from an examination of conditions conducted during the analysis phase of the problem analysis process. They adopt general scientific principles of psychology and mental health to specify the problem.

   Plan tactics include a description of the procedure and materials to be used in treatment plan implementation. This description specifies who will carry out the procedures. The tactics provide a description of the conditions in which treatment implementation will occur and offer a way to translate principles into problem-solving practice.

APPENDIX C

Discussion Questions

The following questions are designed to elicit further considerations in conducting a problem analysis and to promote discussion in group training sessions following the viewing of a problem analysis videotape or a live model.

1. Do you agree with the goals that have been established for the problem(s) identified? What other goals might emerge from a problem analysis?
2. What alternative problem-analysis (measurement) strategies might be used with each problem?
3. What alternative intervention procedures might be used for the problems other than the ones developed by the consultant and the consultee?
4. What possible barriers might be to the implementation of the principles used to solve each problem?
5. What are some alternatives for individuals to carry out the intervention plan given that the identified consultee is unable to?

APPENDIX D

Problem Analysis Interview Record Booklet

Client's name: _____ Sex: _____

Address: _____

_____

School: _____ Grade: _____

Consultant: _____

Consultee: _____

	Year	Month	Day
Date of assessment:	_____	_____	_____
Birthdate:	_____	_____	_____
Age:	_____	_____	_____

Problem Analysis Interview (PAI)

Assessor note: The purposes of the PAI are to:

- Evaluate and obtain agreement on the sufficiency and the adequacy of the baseline data.
- Conduct a tentative functional analysis—discuss the antecedent, consequent, and sequential conditions.
- Discuss and reach agreement on the goal for the behavior change.
- Design an intervention plan, including a specification of the antecedent, situational, or consequent conditions to be changed and of the who, what, and where regarding the change.
- Reaffirm the record-keeping procedure.
- Schedule a problem evaluation interview.

The consultant should question and/or comment on the following areas:

1. Opening salutation

2. General statement about the data and the problem (e.g., "Let's look at the record on Jimmy's hitting")

Record responses: _____

_____

_____

_____

_____

3. Questions or statement about strength of behavior (e.g., "It looks as if Jimmy refused to do the assigned work except on Tuesday")

Record responses: _____

_____

_____

_____

_____

4. Questions about conditions: antecedent, consequent, and sequential (e.g., "Did you notice anything in particular that happened just *before* . . . ?" or "What happened *after* Mary . . . ?" or "What was going on *when* Jimmy . . . ?")

Record responses:

Antecedent: _____

_____

_____

Consequent: _____

_____

_____

Sequential: _____

_____

_____

5. Summarizing statement specifying target behavior, conditions, and strength (e.g., "Let's see, Mary was 'disrespectful' by talking back or used abusive language on 3 days last week. This behavior seemed to be related to comments made by other students. We would like to eliminate this behavior and help her produce more positive comments. Is this right?")

Record responses: _____

_____

_____

_____

6. Question and/or statement interpreting the behavior (e.g., "Why do you think Mary is 'disrespectful'?")

Record responses: _____

_____

_____

_____

7. Questions about the plan (e.g., "We need to try something different. What could be done before Mary makes the abusive remarks?" "What could be done to change the setting in which Charles gets into fights?" "How could we remove the attention from the disruptive behavior?")

Record responses: _____

_____

_____

_____

8. Summarize and validate the plan (e.g., "Then we'll try this . . .")

Record responses: _____

_____

_____

_____

9. Statement on continuing recording procedure (an informal written agreement on the plan, the data recording, etc.)

Record responses: _____

_____

_____

_____

10. Establish date of next appointment

Record response:

Date: _____

Day: _____

Time: _____

Place: _____

11. Closing salutation

Problem Analysis Interview Data Sheet

Date: _____   Observer: _____

Client: _____   Reliability-observer: _____

Consultee: _____   Session #: _____

Consultant: _____

Interview objective	Occurrence	Response
1. Opening salutation	_____	_____
2. General statement	_____	_____
3. Behavior strength	_____	_____
4. Behavior conditions		
a. Antecedent	_____	_____
b. Consequent	_____	_____
c. Sequential	_____	_____
5. Summarize and validate	_____	_____
6. Interpretation	_____	_____
7. Plan statement	_____	_____
8. Summarize and validate	_____	_____
9. Continuing data collection	_____	_____
10. Establish date of next appointment	_____	_____
11. Closing salutation	_____	_____

APPENDIX E

Intervention Rating Profile for Consultee and Client

The purpose of this questionnaire is to obtain information that will aid in the selection of classroom interventions. These interventions will be used by teachers of children with behavior problems. Please circle the number that best describes your agreement or disagreement with each statement.

1. This would be an acceptable intervention for the child's problem behavior.   1 2 3 4 5 6
2. Most teachers would find this intervention appropriate for behavior problems in addition to the one described.   1 2 3 4 5 6
3. This intervention should prove effective in changing the child's problem behavior.   1 2 3 4 5 6
4. I would suggest the use of this intervention to other teachers.   1 2 3 4 5 6
5. The child's behavior problem is severe enough to warrant use of this intervention.   1 2 3 4 5 6
6. Most teachers would find this intervention suitable for the behavior problem described.   1 2 3 4 5 6
7. I would be willing to use this intervention in the classroom setting.   1 2 3 4 5 6
8. This intervention would *not* result in negative side-effects for the child.   1 2 3 4 5 6
9. This intervention would be appropriate for a variety of children.   1 2 3 4 5 6
10. This intervention is consistent with those I have used in classroom settings.   1 2 3 4 5 6
11. The intervention was a fair way to handle the child's problem behavior.   1 2 3 4 5 6
12. This intervention is reasonable for the behavior problem described.   1 2 3 4 5 6
13. I liked the procedures used in this intervention.   1 2 3 4 5 6

14. This intervention was a good way to
    handle this child's behavior problem.   1 2 3 4 5 6
15. Overall, this intervention would be
    beneficial for the child.   1 2 3 4 5 6

Source: Martens and Witt (1982).

Children's Intervention Rating Profile

	I agree	I do not agree
1. The method used to deal with the behavior problem was fair.	+_____+_____+_____+_____+_____+	
2. This child's teacher was too harsh on him.	+_____+_____+_____+_____+_____+	
3. The method used to deal with the behavior may cause problems with this child's friends.	+_____+_____+_____+_____+_____+	
4. There are better ways to handle this child's problem than the one described here.	+_____+_____+_____+_____+_____+	
5. The method used by this teacher would be a good one to use with other children.	+_____+_____+_____+_____+_____+	
6. I like the method used for this child's behavior problem.	+_____+_____+_____+_____+_____+	
7. I think that the method used for this problem would help this child do better in school.	+ + + + +_____+	

Source: Elliott (1986).

4

Treatment Implementation

Objectives

Upon completion of this chapter, the reader should be able to:

1. Describe the roles associated with treatment implementation.
2. Discuss procedures for developing treatment implementation skills.
3. Name and describe the objectives of consultation during treatment implementation.

INTRODUCTION

The third stage in the consultative problem-solving process is treatment implementation. During this stage of consultation, the plan designed in problem analysis is put into operation. The function of consultation during treatment implementation is to maximize the likelihood that a plan put into effect will produce the desired outcome.

PREPARING FOR TREATMENT IMPLEMENTATION

The first stage in the treatment implementation process is making preparations for carrying out the plan. Before implementation can occur, it may be necessary to assign people to various roles, to gather the needed materials, and to train the individuals (e.g., parents and teachers) who will carry out the treatment.

Assigning Implementation Roles

The first step to be taken in preparing for implementation is to assign individuals to the various roles required for carrying out the treatment plan. Four basic roles are associated with treatment plan implementation: (1) treatment director; (2) executor; (3) observer; and (4) skill developer.

The treatment director guides the operation of the plan, makes role assignments, specifies the materials to be used, schedules the activities, and specifies the nature of the activities. The consultee generally assumes this role because he or she has a direct and on-going contact with the client.

A second role required for implementation is that of the treatment plan executor. The plan executor is responsible for carrying out the implementation plan. The consultee also typically assumes the role of executor (e.g., parents, teachers, paraprofessionals, and other socialization agents).

The third role generally needed is that of the behavioral observer. The consultee is often responsible for observing behavior. However, other individuals may assume this role. Parents, children, and their peers can be taught to observe and self-observe data in an accurate fashion.

A final role that is sometimes necessary is that of implementation skill developer. If the treatment plan executor lacks the skills necessary for implementation, these skills must be taught. The consultant usually assumes the role of trainer.

Assembling Implementation Materials

A second step that may be involved in preparing for treatment implementation is gathering the materials needed to carry out the plan. For example, the plan may call for gathering rewards or scoring sheets before implementation. Generally, it is best to keep such materials to a minimum. The consultee is typically responsible for gathering materials.

Developing Implementation Skills

If the plan executor lacks the skills needed to implement the treatment plan, the consultant must help to develop these skills. One skill-training method is to train outside the setting where the implementation will occur. Training experiences can be provided before implementation or throughout implementation. Techniques such as advice, simple directions, role playing, lectures, movies, feedback, and actual modeling of the skills may be used.

Though training outside the situation is often necessary, sometimes training is conducted in the setting in which the intervention will occur. This training usually takes the form of guiding the implementation by various methods. One method is to cue the consultee. Another technique is to model the necessary implementation behaviors. A third technique is to provide feedback and reinforcement to the consultee concerning his or her behavior.

The consultant's decision to train is based on several factors: the executor's need for training, the consultee's willingness to be trained, the likelihood that training will be effective, and the cost of training in terms of time, materials, and resources.

OPERATING THE IMPLEMENTATION PLAN

After all the involved parties have prepared for implementation, the treatment plan is put into effect. At this time, the plan executor(s) carries out the plan designed in the problem analysis. Additionally, provisions are made to monitor the plan and to revise the plan as needed.

Monitoring Treatment Implementation

During treatment implementation, two kinds of monitoring usually occur: monitoring the client's behavior and monitoring the operations that occur in carrying out the treatment plan. Provisions for monitoring client behavior are made during problem identification and problem analysis. The consultee is generally responsible for overseeing and implementing this procedure.

The monitoring operations involved in carrying out the plan are conducted to ensure that the treatment plan is being implemented as designed. It is important to do this as soon as possible to rectify inadequacies. Another reason for monitoring operations is to ensure that the assessment of client performance will take place as designed.

Assessment procedures established during problem identification and used in collecting baseline data should be continued during the implementation of the plan.

The monitoring of operations may occur in several ways. One way is to interview the consultee. Another procedure for monitoring is to deserve the treatment plan in operation. Trained observers may be used, or the consultant may assume this role and, at the same time, provide cues and feedback to the consultee. However, this may require too much time on the part of the consultant, even when done intermittently. As another alternative, the monitoring may be accomplished through self-observation by the consultee. This monitoring, however, does require time and may be unreliable. Unfortunately, there is no way to monitor implementation that will be suitable in all cases. The consultant must consider the purposes to be achieved by monitoring and the cost of the various options in terms of time and resources.

Revising Procedures during Treatment Implementation

If monitoring reveals that the client's behavior is not changing as desired, or that the treatment is not being implemented as designed, changes in the procedures may be necessary. One type of change that may be made during treatment implementation is to make the plan operations agree with the plan design. For example, if the plan calls for reinforcing appropriate behavior and ignoring unwanted behavior, and this is not being done, steps may be taken to ensure proper implementation.

The decision to make the treatment designed and the treatment in operation agree should be based, in part, on observed changes in the client's behavior. If the client is changing as desired, the consultant may not want to alter the procedures even if they don't agree with the plan as designed. If the plan is not working, and if there is a discrepancy between operation and design, a change may be necessary.

Factors that are determined to control the lack of agreement between the plan as designed and the plan as implemented will influence the decision to increase agreement. If there is an apparent failure of communication, the obvious course of action is to clarify communication regarding how the plan is to be implemented and then to do what is necessary to ensure that implementation will go as planned. If the executor seems to lack the skills for proper implementation, more specific training may be necessary.

A second type of revision that may be made during treatment implementation is to alter the original plan. Sometimes it may be necessary to alter the plan because it is not effective in producing desired change. In many cases, only minor adjustments may be required.

CONSULTATION DURING TREATMENT IMPLEMENTATION

During treatment implementation, there is generally no formal interview between the consultant and the consultee. Nevertheless, several tasks must be accomplished if the implementation process is to proceed as intended.

Objectives of Consultation during Treatment Implementation

The goals of consultation during implementation fall into three categories: (1) skill development; (2) monitoring the implementation process; and (3) plan revisions.

Skill-Development Objectives

The first skill-development objective is to determine whether the plan executors have the skills to effectively implement the plan. For example, if reinforcement techniques are to be used, the individuals who will apply the reinforcement must know how and when to do so properly. The consultant must compare the skills needed for treatment implementation with his or her knowledge of the skills the plan executor possesses.

If skill development is required, the second skill-development objective is to decide on the training procedures. As previously mentioned, such factors as the willingness of the consultee to participate in training, the likelihood of results, and the costs should be weighed in the training decision.

The third skill-development objective is to design procedures to enhance skill development. The consultant should gather the materials needed for training, work out the procedures to be used in training, and schedule the training.

The fourth consultation objective related to skill development is implementing the procedures to be used in developing skills. The consultant is usually responsible for carrying out the training, although the training may be assigned to other people.

The final skill-development objective is to evaluate the outcome of the skill training. This evaluation is aimed primarily at determining whether the goals of the training have been achieved.

Monitoring Objectives

One monitoring objective is to decide if data collection is proceeding as intended. This task can be accomplished by examining the consultee's records or the client's actual performance. This examination usually indicates when data are being gathered, how performance is being measured, and what behavior is being observed.

A second monitoring goal is to determine whether plan is proceeding as designed. The consultant is responsible for determining that this objective is being achieved. The monitoring of plans often takes place as part of the process of monitoring the data collection on client behavior.

If the consultant has observed little progress toward the goal, it may be beneficial to question the consultee about the manner in which the plan is being implemented to determine if there have been some implementation inadequacies. On the other hand, if obvious progress is being made, the consultant may assume the plan is being implemented properly.

Revision Objectives

The first revision objective during treatment implementation is to determine if there is a need to make any changes in the plan. The consultant generally determines if the client's behavior is changing as desired. If it is, there is usually no need to change the plan. If the client's behavior is not changing as desired and/or if there is a lack of agreement between the design and the implementation, there is a need for plan revision.

The second consultation objective related to revision is to make a revision plan. Generally, this revision requires the use of plan-design interviewing techniques. Quite often, only minor revisions are needed.

CONSULTATIVE INTERACTIONS DURING TREATMENT IMPLEMENTATION

Although there is no formal interview during plan implementation, several kinds of interactions may occur between the consultant and the participants in consultation.

The Brief Contact

The brief contact is an interaction that lasts no more than a few minutes. Sometimes, a brief contact is made by telephone. However, there are some types of information that must be examined in person (e.g., an examination of the data during the treatment phase). In these cases, a face-to-face contact is best. The brief contact functions to monitor implementation, to assist in plan revision, to check progress by examining the data collected, and to schedule the next meeting.

The Observation

A second kind of interaction during treatment implementation is the observation. Observations may be conducted by either the consultant or a trained observer in the treatment setting. Observations may serve to monitor implementation, to develop plan-executor skills, and to develop revisions in treatment implementation.

Training Session(s)

The final type of interaction during plan implementation is the training session conducted outside the treatment setting. The primary function of training is to develop plan-executor skills. An effective training program has several characteristics. First, the general, subordinate, and performance objectives should be delineated. Second, a set of procedures must be specified that indicate how the training is to occur. Third, measures that can be used to see if training goals are being reached should be devised. Training sessions should generally be short. The final matter to be taken up in training is to establish when the next session will occur.

Basically, the plan implementation phase of behavior consultation involves putting the plan developed during problem analysis into operation. Clearly, the effectiveness of consultation depends directly on what is done during plan implementation. The best plan may not produce the desired results if it is not implemented properly.

APPENDIX A
Reading Quiz

1. The function of consultation during implementation is to _____

    _____

    _____ .

2. The treatment implementation director is responsible for the following:

    a. _____

    b. _____

    c. _____

    d. _____

    e. _____

3. In addition to the treatment implementation director, other roles associated with plan implementation are the

    (a) _____, the (b) _____,

    and the (c) _____ .

4. State the techniques that may be used when skill development training occurs during implementation: _____

    _____

    _____ .

5. When monitoring reveals that the behavior is not changing as desired, the consultant may:

    a. _____

    b. _____

6. State the skill development objectives of consultation during treatment implementation:

    a. _____

b. _____

c. _____

d. _____

e. _____

7. State the treatment-implementation monitoring objectives:

a. _____

b. _____

8. State the implementation revision objectives:

a. _____

b. _____

9. State the type of consultative interactions that may occur during treatment implementation:

a. _____

b. _____

c. _____

APPENDIX B

Reading Quiz Answers

1. maximize the likelihood that the plan will be effective.
2. a. Guiding the implementation
   b. Making the role assignments
   c. Scheduling the activities
   d. Specifying the materials
   e. Specifying the nature of the activities
3. (a) plan executor
   (b) behavioral observer
   (c) skill developer
4. Advice, verbal directions, lectures, videos, role playing, modeling, feedback, reinforcement, and cuing.
5. a. revise the implementation to make treatment plan operations agree with the plan design.
   b. alter the original plan.
6. a. Determining whether the consultant possesses the skills needed for implementation
   b. Ascertaining the feasibility of training
   c. Designing the procedures
   d. Implementing the procedures
   e. Evaluating the outcome and the procedures
7. a. Monitoring the data collection
   b. Monitoring the treatment plan operations
8. a. Determining the need for revision
   b. Developing a revised plan when the need for revision exists
9. a. The brief contact
   b. The observation
   c. The training session

APPENDIX C

Discussion Questions

The following questions are designed to elicit further considerations in treatment implementation and to promote discussion in group training sessions following the reading of this chapter.

1. What are some training options for consultees who participate in consultation?
2. Describe some in-service training-program activities that can assist consultees who are involved in consultation services.

5

Treatment Evaluation

On completion of this chapter, the reader should be able to:

1. Describe how goal attainment is evaluated.
2. Describe the factors influencing judgments of congruence between objectives and behavior in problem-centered and developmental consultation.
3. Describe courses of action related to the judgmental categories of no progress toward the goal, progress toward the goal, partial attainment of the goal, and goal attainment.
4. Discuss postimplementation treatment-plan alternatives.

INTRODUCTION

After a treatment plan has been in effect for a suitable period, treatment evaluation is undertaken to determine whether the goals of consultation have been attained, whether the plan implemented has been effective, and whether the treatment has been acceptable to consultee and client. The information provided through formal treatment evaluation makes it possible for the parties involved in the consultation process to determine what course of action to take next. Treatment evaluation may indicate that consultation should be continued or terminated, or that a postimplementation treatment plan (i.e., generalization and maintenance) should be put into effect. An evaluation of the acceptability of the treatment may indicate that other procedures need to be considered. This evaluation may be especially helpful if a revision in the treatment plan is being made or in future contacts with the consultee and the client. The evaluation process includes evaluating goal attainment, evaluating plan effectiveness, and postimplementation planning.

EVALUATING GOAL ATTAINMENT

The first step in treatment evaluation is to determine whether the goals of consultation have been achieved. This determination provides the necessary information for making decisions concerning future actions to be taken in regard to client behavior. For example, in a treatment plan designed to decrease arguing among siblings, it may be determined that the goals of consultation have not been met and that an alteration in the plan itself should be made.

Judging Congruence between Objectives and Behavior

The process of evaluating goal attainment begins during problem identification with the specification of the objectives and of procedures for measuring their mastery. Data collected on client behavior during consultation provide the information that is needed to judge the congruence between the objectives and performance.

In the case of problem-centered consultation, judgments of congruence between objectives and behavior are based on an examination of the data collected on client behavior in relation to the goals that were established during problem identification. If client behavior matches the standard established during problem identification, goal attainment has occurred. If behavior does not match the required performance level, the goal has not been attained.

The judgment of congruence between performance objectives and performance in developmental consultation is the same as in problem-centered consultation. The congruence between behavior and a subordinate objective is established by determining whether all the performance goals within the subordinate objectives have been achieved. The congruence between behavior and a general objective is achieved when all the subordinate objectives included within the general objective have been mastered.

Making Decisions on the Basis of Congruence

A determination of the congruence between behavior and objectives provides the feedback necessary to guide decision making in consultation. The judgment of congruence may be described in terms of three categories: (1) no progress toward goal; (2) some progress toward goal; and (3) goal attained. Each category suggests a different course of action.

The most unfortunate outcome in consultation is no progress

toward goals. When this occurs, the first course of action is to return to problem analysis. The consultant should focus initially on determining whether the plan was implemented as intended. If the plan was not implemented as designed, it should be implemented when feasible, or suitable alternatives should be devised. If the plan was implemented as designed, the focus should shift to reconsidering the factors that may be controlling the client's behavior. A new plan based on these factors should then be devised to facilitate goal attainment.

In cases where there is no progress toward the goal, consultation may terminate. If it seems unlikely that the initial goal can be achieved, the consultee may decide that it is useless to proceed. In such cases, the consultant may decide to treat the client directly or to consider alternative services.

Another alternative that may be pursued when there has been no progress toward the goal is to return to problem identification and to redefine the goal of consultation. On the other hand, even though the initial goal of consultation is apparently unattainable, a revised goal may be reached. For example, the initial aim of consultation may be to assist a male child to complete academic assignments within a given time period. Suppose that, in such a case, problem evaluation reveals no progress toward goal attainment, yet problem analysis has revealed that the child possesses the skills necessary to complete the assignments. The difficulty may be simply that the child cannot do the work as quickly as desired. Under these conditions, the consultant and the consultee may choose to revise the goal of consultation so that the child has some chance of reaching it. After the child has experienced some success with the revised goal, more stringent performance requirements may be introduced.

In some cases, though the goal of consultation has not been attained, there is some progress toward the goal. The course of action to be taken depends on the kind of objective with which one is dealing. In the case of a behavioral goal or a performance objective, partial goal attainment suggests a return to problem analysis. The consultee and the consultant should consider whether the treatment plan should be maintained or revised. When there is steady progress toward the goal, the initial plan may be left in operation.

In the case of subordinate objectives, partial goal attainment is an important issue for consultation when not all performance objectives have been considered. This state of affairs indicates a need to return to problem identification. During successive problem-evaluation interviews in developmental consultation, the consultant and the consultee must determine whether subordinate goals have been achieved. If they have not, a return to problem identification is warranted. For example, the general objective for a child may be to increase social interactions. Although the subordinate objectives of increased frequency of verbal interactions with peers during preschool hours and increased eye contact with teachers may have been accomplished, the frequency of social interactions at home may not have changed. Thus, it would be advisable to return to problem identification to specify precisely the behaviors and conditions of concern in that setting.

As in the case of subordinate objectives, partial goal attainment for general objectives calls for a return to problem identification. For example, suppose that there are three subordinate objectives for a given general objective and two have been mastered. Problem identification would be undertaken to identify the performance objectives for the third goal or to gather data on the mastery of the performance objectives if they have already been specified.

In some cases, consultation may terminate following partial attainment of behavioral, subordinate, or general goals if the consultee feels that continued improvement is likely and no further sessions are needed. When the goals of consultation have been achieved, the consultant should proceed to the next phase in the problem evaluation process.

EVALUATING PLAN EFFECTIVENESS

The second step of the treatment evaluation process is the evaluation of the plan's effectiveness. Information concerning plan effectiveness may not always directly influence decision making with respect to the case at hand, but it may be useful for solving future problems of a similar nature. The task of evaluating plan effectiveness is to select and implement an appropriate evaluative design. An evaluation design specifies when observations of client behavior will take place and when plan implementation will occur in relation to these observations.

Plan evaluation may involve any of a broad range of designs developed for clinical experimental research. The reader is directed to several sources for a detailed discussion of time-series designs (Barlow, Hayes, & Nelson, 1984; Barlow & Hersen, 1984; Jayaratne & Levy, 1979; Kazdin, 1982; Kratochwill, 1978). Barlow *et al.* (1984) and Jayaratne and Levy (1979) are especially useful sources for the evaluation of clinical practice.

The simplest design is the basic time-series design, or AB design. This evaluation design involves the collection of baseline data over a series of points in time. Intervention then occurs, and a second set of observations is made. Figure 5.1 shows a graphic example of an AB design. The basic time-series design is widely used because of its ease of application. The application of the design requires only that baseline data be collected following the problem identification interview and that data collection continue during plan implementation. The

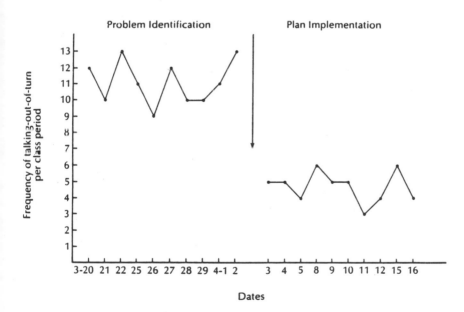

FIGURE 5.1. An example of an AB design used to evaluate consultation outcomes. (Source: J. R. Bergan & T. R. Kratochwill (1990). *Behavioral consultation and therapy.* New York: Plenum Press.)

basic problem with the AB design is that it does not control for the possibility that an event occurring at the same time as the intervention may have produced the changes in behavior. There are numerous other evaluation designs that can be used in consultation, but these procedures are not reviewed here. The consultant interested in other design and evaluation alternatives used in consultation should review Bergan and Kratochwill (1990).

POSTIMPLEMENTATION PLANNING

Postimplementation planning is the final step in problem evaluation. It is undertaken to ensure that a problem will not occur again and to alert the consultant if it does.

Postimplementation Plan Alternatives

Basically, three alternatives are available for designing a postimplementation plan. One alternative is to leave the present plan in effect, especially if it is likely that the client's behavior can be easily reversed. A second alternative in postimplementation planning is to introduce a new plan after consultation has been terminated. A new plan may be needed to maintain the behavior change when the behavior is reversible and it is impractical to leave the original plan in operation. Another circumstance that calls for implementing a new plan is that in which there is a need to ensure that the behavior change will generalize to new settings.

Several strategies can be used in designing a postimplementation plan to ensure the maintenance and generalization of behavior changed in consultation. Stokes and Baer (1977) reviewed some categories that directly related to a technology of generalization:

1. *Natural maintaining contingencies* involves a strategy in which generalization may be programmed by suitable trapping manipulations. Likewise, responses are introduced to natural reinforcement contingencies that refine and maintain those skills without further treatment.

2. In *training sufficient exemplars*, generalization to untrained stimulus conditions and to untrained responses is programmed by the

training of sufficient exemplars to those stimulus conditions or responses.

3. *Train loosely* is a programming technique in which training is considered with relatively little control over the stimuli and responses involved, and generalization is thereby enhanced.

4. In *indiscriminable contingencies*, reinforcement contingencies, or the setting events marking the presence or absence of those contingencies, are deliberately made less predictable, so that it becomes difficult to discriminate reinforcement occasions from nonreinforcement occasions.

5. *Common stimuli* are used in generalization programming by incorporating into training settings those social and physical stimuli that are salient in generalization settings and that can be made to assume functional or obvious roles in the training setting.

6. *Mediated generalization* requires establishing a response as part of new learning that is likely to be used in other problem situations, and therefore to result in generalization.

7. *Training "to generalize"* involves reinforcing generalization itself as if it were an explicit behavior.

The final alternative available in postimplementation planning is to remove the treatment plan implemented during consultation. This may be done gradually or all at once. The safest circumstance for removing the treatment plan is when the behaviors of concern are not easily reversible and contingencies operating in the natural environment will maintain the behavior. An implicit purpose of behavior change programs is to increase the availability of reinforcement for desired behaviors. When this has been accomplished through consultation, it is often possible to remove the plan.

Postimplementation Recording

It is generally useful to include some provision for postimplementation recording. Postimplementation records provide the necessary data for judging whether behavior changes have been maintained or generalized to new settings. Such recording should, however, be kept to a minimum and should be made as easy as possible.

One strategy for postimplementation recording is the probe technique, which involves periodic measures under conditions that are set up during postimplementation planning. One way to use the probe technique is to assess behavior over a fixed sequence of times to verify the durability of the behavior change. A second way to probe is to assess behavior under varying conditions at different times.

Postimplementation Treatment Acceptability

As noted in Chapter 3, the consultant should consider conducting an assessment of the treatment's acceptability during the problem analysis phase of consultation. Assessment of treatment acceptability during this phase may increase the probability that the treatment will be implemented correctly. It is also useful to assess treatment acceptability after the consultee and the client have had experience with the treatment. In such cases, the same assessment formats should be used to compare acceptability before and after treatment. (Again, the IRP-15 and the CIRP are recommended; see Appendix E, Chapter 3.)

Essentially, four possible outcomes may occur in a consideration of effectiveness and acceptability: acceptable and effective treatment, acceptable but not effective treatment, not acceptable but effective treatment, or not acceptable or effective treatment. The consultant must consider each outcome and maximize the acceptable and effective outcome for consultee and client.

Postimplementation and Problem Recurrence

Despite the consultant's and the consultee's best effort, problems may recur after the termination of consultation. The negative effects of problem recurrence can be forestalled if steps are taken to ensure the formulation of a new plan to deal with new problems. The postimplementation treatment plan needs to provide for contact between the consultant and the consultee to deal with problem recurrence. In the case of developmental consultation, periodic postimplementation evaluations should be scheduled during the problem evaluation interviews conducted. These should be conducted in reiterative applications of the problem-solving process.

Contact regarding postimplementation evaluations are more difficult to ensure in problem-solving consultation and must be planned systematically. One way to arrange for contact is for the consultant to encourage the consultee to make contact in the event that a problem recurs. An alternative method is for the consultant to initiate the contact. This technique ensures that contact will be made and is an indication to the consultee that the consultant is ready to provide assistance if required.

In many cases, it may be useful to provide for contact by making a contingency plan during treatment evaluation. The contingency plan should specify the procedures to be implemented in the event of problem recurrence. An obvious contingency plan would be to re-institute the original plan in the event of problem recurrence.

THE TREATMENT EVALUATION INTERVIEW

In the treatment evaluation interview, the consultee and consultant determine whether the goals of consultation have been attained. Based on this determination, they decide whether there is a need for further problem identification or problem analysis. Finally, if the goal has been attained, postimplementation plans are made to reduce the likelihood of problem recurrence and to deal with problem recurrence.

Interview objectives for problem-centered and developmental consultation fall into five categories: (1) goal attainment; (2) consultation guidance; (3) plan effectiveness; (4) postimplementation planning; and (5) procedural.

Goal Attainment Objectives for Developmental Consultation

The first task of the consultant in the treatment evaluation interview is to establish the extent to which the goals of consultation have been reached. In the case of developmental consultation, this requires the consideration of general, subordinate, and performance objectives. At first, the evaluation may center only on performance and subordinate objectives.

The consultant should begin by considering the performance objectives targeted during the plan implementation period preceding the evaluation interview. Each objective should be dealt with separately. The consultant should first start by examining the data and summarizing the objectives as established during problem identification. Next, he or she should summarize the data from the treatment plan implementation. Finally, the consultant should ask the consultee for his or her judgment of the extent of goal attainment. When all phases of evaluation have been taken up for the first performance objective, an evaluation of goal attainment is initiated for another objective. This process is continued until all performance objectives have been considered. After all performance objectives have been discussed, an evaluation of goal attainment is undertaken for subordinate objectives.

The evaluation of a performance objective is initiated by summarizing the objective as it was stated during problem identification. Next, the consultant recounts the performance objectives included within the subordinate goal. Any additional performance objectives to be included within the subordinate objective(s) are then specified. The consultant then summarizes the status of the previously specified performance goals with respect to goal attainment. Finally, if the data suggest that the subordinate goal has been attained, the consultant asks the consultee for his or her judgment of whether the subordinate goal has been attained. If goal attainment has been reached for a particular subordinate objective, the discussion turns to a second subordinate objective. The evaluation proceeds as with the first subordinate objective.

During the latter stages of developmental consultation, consideration must be given to evaluating the attainment of the general objectives. The consultant begins by summarizing the objective as it was stated during problem identification. The consultant then summarizes the status of each subordinate goal with respect to the issue of goal attainment. Finally, the consultant asks the consultee to make a judgment on the attainment of the general goal.

Goal Attainment Objectives for Problem-Centered Consultation

The only goal attainment objective for problem-centered consultation is to determine the extent to which the behavioral goals established during problem identification have been achieved. The consultant begins by selecting one of the behavioral goals, examining the data, and summarizing the goal as it was established during problem identification. The consultant should then summarize the data collected during the plan implementation. The final step is to ask the consultee to judge the goal attainment.

After goal attainment has been evaluated for the first goal, the discussion should shift to the next phase of the evaluation interview. When all phases of the evaluation for the initial goal have been completed, another goal should be considered through the same process. When all the goals have been evaluated, the interview is completed.

Consultation Guidance Objectives

The term *consultation guidance objectives* indicates interview goals related to guiding the consultant on the basis of feedback concerning goal attainment. One of the tasks of the consultant at this point is to signal the need either to progress to the next phase of evaluation or to go back to an earlier stage in the process. If goal attainment has not occurred, it may be necessary to go back to problem identification or problem analysis. The consultant should use the guidelines discussed previously to determine the proper cause of action.

Postimplementation Planning Objectives

The first interview goal in postimplementation planning is to select a postimplementation plan alternative from among the three possible types of plans that may be put into operation following the termination of consultation. A discussion of the alternatives may be initiated by alerting the consultee to the need for decision making concerning the advisability of leaving the plan in effect, removing the plan, or constructing a new plan. The consultant may wish to point out factors that may influence the likelihood of problem recurrence.

When all the factors relevant to problem recurrence have been discussed, the consultant should ask the consultee to select a postimplementation plan alternative. If the consultee chooses either to leave the implemented plan in effect following consultation or to remove the plan, the discussion is complete. However, if the choice is to construct a new plan or to phase out the old, new plan strategies and tactics should be established.

When a postimplementation plan has been established, provision must be made for recording. The consultant is usually responsible for developing recording procedures. The procedures described in Chapter 2 should be followed.

The final objective in postimplementation recording is to establish procedures that specify what to do if the problem recurs. The consultant may plan for contact either by requesting the consultee to initiate contact if the problem should reappear or by suggesting a consultant-initiated contact.

Procedural Objectives in Treatment Evaluation

The first procedural objective in treatment evaluation is to schedule additional interviews if one or more of the goals have not been attained. The second procedural objective is to terminate consultation if all goals have been attained.

Treatment-Evaluation-Interview Example

The following is an example of a treatment evaluation interview:

Consultant: Okay, how did it go?

Consultee: Well, it's not working!

Consultant: It's not working! What do the data look like?

Consultee: It looks as if it hasn't made any difference in the number of times that he's talking.

Consultant: How often, did he talk any more last week? How often did he talk?

Consultee: Just about three times. That's about it.

Consultant: Three times in the whole week?

Consultee: Yes.

Consultant: So it's . . .

Consultee: It looks as if it's not having any effect.

Consultant: Okay, we have to do something else. I think that we need to try something that's more powerful.

Consultee: Uh-huh.

Consultant: What we did was indirect. I think we need to try something that's more powerful. Is there anything around the school that Walter especially likes?

Consultee: You mean activities or something like that?

Consultant: Are there any privileges around school or special materials that he especially likes?

Consultee: We do let different children start the line. That's a privilege that the children usually like. And then there are different chores we let the children do, and we change it so that different ones get a turn; everybody gets a turn to do them.

Consultant: Does Walter like to do those things? Does he like to do the chores?

Consultee: Well, he does them when we ask him to. I'm not really sure if he likes it or not. It's hard to tell. He does it, but I'm not sure if he likes it that much.

Consultant: What about lining up first?

Consultee: I think he likes that. The problem with that would be that, if we let him do it all the time, I don't think that would be good for the other children because they all like it so much. I don't think that would be a good idea.

Consultant: Is there anything else around school, something that Walter could get or have, say, if he talked?

Consultee: Well, those are about the only privileges, and they're all rotated. I could do something like give him a piece of candy or something like that when he talks.

Consultant: You could do that? You could give him candy?

Consultee: Sure.

Consultant: That would be really good. Maybe you could do this. I'm thinking that what we need to do is more teaching. Could you do this: A couple of times during the day—say, when Walter comes to school—could you go up to Walter and say, "Walter, if you say 'hi,' I'll give you whatever, a piece of candy or a raisin, or a piece of popcorn, or a sunflower seed"? A lot of children like sunflower seeds. I mean it doesn't have to be candy. A lot of children like other things besides candy. Sometimes, people don't like to use candy, but there are lots of things like that.

Consultee: Sure, we could try that.

Consultant: Okay, say five times a day?

Consultee: That I should go up to him and ask him to say something and give him a piece of candy, you mean?

Consultant: Right.

Consultee: I don't think five times a day would be a problem. I'd be able to do that, I think.

Consultant: Okay. Let's do that. Let's practice that.

Consultee: Okay. When should I do it? Should I go ahead and tell him that he's going to get the candy when he says something, or should I just give him the candy when he says it?

Consultant: You might want to explain it to Walter ahead of time, then go up to Walter and say, "Walter, if you say . . ." and I would stick to one word. Other children say, "Teacher, look at what I have." You could say . . .

Consultee: You mean just ask him to say one word?

Consultant: Right.

Consultee: But not the same word all the time.

Consultant: No, right. Different words. But say, "Walter, if you say 'look,' I'll give you a raisin."

Consultee: Uh-huh. Okay.

Consultant: Okay?

Consultee: Yes.

Consultant: And then you could do the same thing when he comes up to get some kind of materials.

Consultee: Uh-huh.

Consultant: When he comes up and wants his shoes tied.

Consultee: When he points to something.

Consultant: Right. When he points, you could say, "Walter, if you say 'paint,' I'll give you the paint . . ."

Consultee: Okay.

Consultant: ". . . and I'll give you a raisin." Okay, let's practice that.

Consultee: Okay.

Consultant: Okay. I'll be you and you be Walter.

Consultee: Alright. I'll be Walter?

Consultant: Right, you be Walter, and why don't you come up and you want your shoes tied. Okay? Walter, if you say "tie," I'll tie your shoes and give you a raisin.

Consultee: Tie.

Consultant: Good, Walter, that's good. Here's your raisin.

TREATMENT EVALUATION   173

Consultee: Okay, should I tell him that's good when I do it?

Consultant: Yes, why don't you do that?

Consultee: What if he doesn't do it? You know, what if he doesn't do it the first time? What should I do?

Consultant: Just go back to your work.

Consultee: And what if he comes and shows me his shoe again?

Consultant: Just . . .

Consultee: Same thing?

Consultant: Same thing.

Consultee: Okay.

Consultant: What you don't want to get into is "Walter, say 'tie,' Walter, say 'tie,' Walter, say 'tie' and I'll give you a raisin. Do you want a raisin, Walter?" That's what you don't want to do.

Consultee: So you just want me to say it once, and if he doesn't do it, forget it?

Consultant: Right.

Consultee: Okay.

Consultant: Now you be you and I'll be Walter.

Consultee: All right.

Consultant: Okay?

Consultee: Walter, if you say "tie" I'll give you a raisin. (*No response.*) Now I don't know what to do with that.

Consultant: Just ignore it. Go back to your work.

Consultee: Okay.

Consultant: You go ahead and ignore it.

Consultee: Okay.

Consultant: Okay?

Consultee: All right.

Consultant: Okay, and can you continue to collect the same kind of data?

Consultee: Counting how many times? Yes.

Consultant: Right.

Consultee: Do you want me to still take it on Dewey?

Consultant: Yes. Can I tell you on Friday and see how it's going?

Consultee: Yes, Friday would be fine.

Consultant: Then I'll call on Friday, and we can set up another meeting if it looks as if we need one then.

Consultee: Okay. So I should forget about the other thing and just do this asking him to say just one word?

Consultant: Okay?

Consultee: Uh-huh. Hope it works.

Discussion of the Interview Transcript

The treatment evaluation interview revealed immediately that the goal of consultation had not been achieved. The data collected by the consultee did not show any improvement whatever in the child's performance. Accordingly, the consultant had to decide what to do next. As discussed previously, when there has been no progress toward goal attainment, the first course of action that the consultant should consider is a return to problem analysis. The consultant elected this option in Walter's case.

The plan formulated during the return to the problem analysis took into consideration the information gleaned about the conditions surrounding Walter's lack of speech during problem identification. During the second problem analysis, the consultant realized that, because talking was a low-rate behavior for Walter, it would have to be cued in order to occur. It is well known that it is very difficult to increase low-rate responses when no procedures other than reinforcement are used to elicit the responses of interest (Bandura, 1969). When the consultant took this fact into account, she began to look for cues that could be used to elicit verbal behavior from Walter. The teacher had mentioned a number of these during problem identification. For example, she pointed out that requests for materials and requests for assistance in tying his shoes were situations that the teacher regarded as cues for Walter to speak. The teacher had previously emitted verbal cues to Walter requesting speech in these situations, but to no avail. Nevertheless, the consultant realized that these verbal and situational cues could be used as part of a plan to increase the frequency of Walter's verbalizations. For example, the consultant suggested that, when Walter wanted materials such as paints, the consultee ask him to make his request in words.

During the first problem-analysis interview, the consultant had taken the position that it would be necessary to reinforce speech behavior to increase it. The major difference between the first plan and the second was that, in the second plan, reinforcement was coupled with cuing. In addition, Walter was told that positive consequences would follow verbal behavior. For instance, the consultant suggested that the teacher might say, "If you say 'paint,' I'll give you the paint . . . and I'll give you a raisin."

The reinforces selected to increase Walter's speaking behavior included the consequences that the teacher had mentioned as consequent conditions during problem identification. In addition, to the consultant's surprise, the teacher suggested the use of food as a reinforcer. It might have been possible to produce the desired changes in Walter's behavior without using food. There would have been some advantage to avoiding the use of food, as the other reinforcers in the situation were ones that were typically associated with cues for Walter to speak. The application of food required that the teacher carry raisins or other goodies with her. This would not have been necessary if only the reinforcers already available in the situation (natural reinforcers) had been applied.

A particularly significant feature of the second plan was that it required the teacher to ignore nonverbal communications aimed at eliciting reinforcers that were being used to increase verbal behavior. For example, the teacher was advised to ignore Walter's nonverbal requests for materials or assistance in tying his shoes. Thus, whereas during problem identification Walter had been able to get the things that he wanted through the use of gestures, during the implementation of the second plan he had to speak if he was to get what he wanted.

The second analysis is of interest not only because it demonstrates the construction of a plan that was potentially far superior to the plan initially put into effect, but also because it illustrates the use of role playing as a technique for training plan executors in consultation. Role playing had been found to be an effective tool for training the individuals responsible for carrying out a plan to implement the plan correctly. In this case, the consultant demonstrated the fact that role playing can be incorporated directly into a consultation interview when desired (see Bergan & Kratochwill, 1990, for further discussion of this issue).

A second problem-evaluation interview revealed that the goal of consultation has been attained and suggested that the plan designed to achieve the goal was effective. As is often the case in consultation, an AB design was used. Thus, the conclusion that the plan produced the desired outcome that was observed is subject to the limitations discussed earlier with respect to validity. Of particular importance in this regard is the fact that history cannot be ruled out as a possible source of influence on Walter's behavior. It is possible that some extraneous event occurring at the time of the plan implementation was responsible for the observed increase in Walter's verbalizations.

APPENDIX A
Reading Quiz

1. Goal attainment is evaluated based on judgments concerning the congruence between (a) _____ and (b) _____

_____.

2. The goal attainment evaluation process begins during (a) _____

_____ with the specification of (b) _____

_____ and procedures for (c) _____.

3. In developmental consultation, congruence between objectives and behavior is judged by assessing _____

_____.

4. List three possible decisions to be made when there has been no progress toward goal attainment:

a. _____

b. _____

c. _____

5. Discuss the phases in the AB design and its major shortcomings:

_____

_____

_____

_____

6. List and discuss three postimplementation-plan alternatives:

a. _____

_____

_____

_____

b. _____

_____

_____

_____

c. _____

_____

_____

_____

APPENDIX B
Reading Quiz Answers

1. (a) objectives
   (b) current performance.
2. (a) problem identification
   (b) objectives
   (c) measuring mastery.
3. the extent to which behavior is congruent with the general, subordinate, and performance objectives established during problem identification.
4. a. Return to problem analysis and focus on determining whether the plan has been implemented as intended; if it has, reconsider the factors that may control the behavior.
   b. Terminate.
   c. Return to problem identification and redefine the goal in more basic steps.
5. The AB design consists of a baseline and an intervention phase. The baseline phase (A) refers to the repeated measurement of the target behavior before treatment. The intervention phase (B) involves repeated measurement following the introduction of the treatment. The major limitation of the AB design is that the consultant cannot determine completely that the observed effect is due only to the intervention.
6. a. Leave the plan in effect if the consultee's behavior is easily reversed or if it is practical.
   b. Introduce a new plan if the behavior is reversible and the original plan is impractical.
   c. Remove the plan. The plan may be removed gradually or all at once. The plan may be removed all at once if the behavior is not likely to reverse and if there is a likelihood that the natural environment will maintain it.

APPENDIX C

Discussion Questions

The following questions are designed to elicit further considerations and promote discussion in group training sessions following the viewing of a treatment evaluation videotape or a live model.

1. For the problem identified and analyzed, do you believe that goal attainment has been achieved?
2. What are some advantages of the effectiveness of the plan success?
3. What are some possible directions for the next problem identification?
4. What things may be done by the consultant and the consultee to ensure that the success achieved will be maintained?
5. What are the implications for the teacher with successful resolution of the problem?

APPENDIX D

Treatment Evaluation Interview Record Booklet

Client name: _____ Sex: _____

Address: _____

_____

School: _____ Grade: _____

Consultant: _____

Consultee: _____

	Year	Month	Day
Date of assessment:	_____	_____	_____
Birthdate:	_____	_____	_____
Age:	_____	_____	_____

Treatment Evaluation Interview (TEI)

Consultant note: The purposes of the TEI are to:

- Determine if the goals of consultation have been obtained.
- Evaluate the effectiveness of the treatment plan.
- Discuss strategies and tactics regarding the continuation, modification, or termination of the treatment plan.
- Schedule additional interviews if necessary or terminate consultation.

The consultant should question and/or comment in the following areas:

1. Opening salutation
2. Evaluate goal attainment: Questions about outcome (e.g., "How did things go?")

Record responses: _____

_____

_____

3. Questions about goal attainment (e.g., "Is Charles completing his work now?" or "Can we say that the goal of increasing Charles's work completion has been attained now?")

Record responses: _____

_____

_____

4. Evaluate plan effectiveness: Questions regarding internal validity of plan (e.g., "Would you say that the contract procedure was responsible for reducing John's profane language?")

Record responses: _____

_____

_____

5. Evaluate external validity of plan (e.g., "Do you think this plan would have worked with another student?")

Record responses: _____

_____

_____

6. Conduct postimplementation planning: Questions and statements regarding plan continuation (e.g., "Do you want to leave the point system in effect for another week to see if John's progress continues?" or "Perhaps we should continue the DRL program for another week")

Record responses: _____

_____

_____

7. Questions and statements regarding plan modification (e.g., "You are saying that you want to discontinue the contract procedure because it has worked so well" or "How could we change the reinforcement procedure to make our plan more effective?" or "Perhaps you could reinforce more frequently")

Record responses: _____

_____

_____

8. Design procedures to facilitate generalization and maintenance (e.g., "What procedures can be implemented to be sure that Sally continues to finish her housework?")

Record responses: _____

_____

_____

9. Arrange for follow-up assessment (e.g., "Now that we have success in the program for George, how can we monitor his progress in the future?")

Record responses: _____

_____

_____

10. Arrange for subsequent interviews or terminate consultation: Questions and statements regarding future interviews (e.g., "When can we get together again to discuss Gwen's progress under our new plan?" or "We probably need to meet again next week to discuss our new plan")

Record responses: _____

_____

_____

11. Statements regarding termination of consultation (e.g., "Since our goals for Bob have been met, this will be the last time we need

to meet unless you have further concerns" or "If you have further problems, please feel free to call on me")

Record responses: _____

_____

_____

12. Closing salutation

Treatment Evaluation Interview Data Sheet

Date: _____   Observer: _____

Client script: _____   Reliability observer: _____

Consultant: _____   Session #: _____

Interview objective	Occurrence	Response
1. Opening salutation	_____	_____
2. Outcome questions	_____	_____
3. Goal attainment questions	_____	_____
4. Internal validity	_____	_____
5. External validity	_____	_____
6. Plan continuation	_____	_____
7. Plan modification validation	_____	_____
8. Generalization and maintenance	_____	_____
9. Follow-up assessment	_____	_____
10. Future interviews	_____	_____
11. Termination of consultation	_____	_____
12. Closing salutation	_____	_____

References

Adler, A. (1964). *Social interest: A challenge to mankind*. New York: Capricorn Books.

Argyris, C. (1964). *Integrating the individual and the organization*. New York: Wiley.

Association for the Advancement of Behavior Therapy. (1977). Ethical issues for human services. *Behavior Therapy, 8*, v–vi.

Bandura, A. (1969). *Principles of behavior modification*. New York: Holt, Rinehart, & Winston.

Barlow, D. H., & Hersen, M. (1984). *Single case experimental designs: Strategies for studying behavior change* (2nd ed). New York: Pergamon Press.

Barlow, D. H., Hayes, S. C., & Nelson, R. O. (1984). *The scientist practitioner: Research and accountability in clinical and educational settings*. New York: Pergamon Press.

Bennis, W. G. (1969). *Changing organizations*. New York: McGraw-Hill.

Bennis, W. G. (1970). *Beyond bureaucracy*. New York: McGraw-Hill.

Bergan, J. R. (1977). *Behavioral consultation*. Columbus, OH: Charles E. Merrill.

Bergan, J. R., & Kratochwill, T. R. (1990). *Behavioral consultation and therapy*. New York: Plenum Press.

Bergan, J. R., & Tombari, M. L. (1975). The analysis of verbal interactions occurring during consultation. *Journal of School Psychology, 13*, 209–226.

Bergan, J. R., & Tombari, M. L. (1976). Consultant skill and efficiency and the implementation of outcomes of consultation. *Journal of School Psychology, 14*, 3–14.

Brown, D., Wyne, M. D., Blackburn, J. E., & Powell, W. C. (1979). *Consultation: Strategy for improving education*. Boston: Allyn & Bacon.

Caplan, G. (1970). *The theory and practice of mental health consultation*. New York: Basic Books.

Chesler, M. A., Bryant, B. I., Jr., & Crowfoot, J. E. (1981). Consultation in schools: Inevitable conflict, partisanship, and advocacy. In M. J. Curtis & J. E. Zins (Eds.), *The theory and practice of school consultation*. Springfield, IL: Charles C Thomas.

Conoley, J. C., & Conoley, C. W. (1982). *School consultation: A guide to practice and training*. New York: Pergamon Press.

Donnellan, A. M., Mirenda, P. A., Mesaros, R. A., & Fassbender, L. L. (1984). Analyzing the communicative functions of aberrant behavior. *Journal of the Association for the Severely Handicapped, 9,* 201–212.

Dreikurs, R. (1948). *The challenge of parenthood.* New York: Duell, Sloan & Pearce.

Dreikurs, R. (1967). *Psychology in the classroom* (2nd ed.). New York: Harper & Row.

Elliott, S. N. (1986). Children's ratings of the acceptability of classroom interventions for misbehavior: Findings and methodological considerations. *Journal of School Psychology, 24,* 23–35.

Fehrenbach, P. A., & Thelen, M. H. (1982). Behavioral approaches to aggressive disorders. *Behavior Modification, 6,* 465–477.

Gallessich, J. (1982). *The profession and practice of consultation.* San Francisco: Jossey-Bass.

Gallessich, J. (1985). Toward a meta-theory of consultation. *The Counseling Psychologist, 13,* 336–354.

Gardner, N. (1974). Action training and research: Something old and something new. *Public Administration Review, 34,* 106–115.

Gelfand, D. M., & Hartmann, D. P. (1984). *Child behavior: Analysis and therapy* (2nd ed). Elmsford, NY: Pergamon Press.

Hartmann, D. P. (1984). Assessment strategies. In D. H. Barlow & M. Hersen (Eds.), *Single case experimental designs: Strategies for studying behavior change* (2nd ed.). New York: Pergamon Press.

Hawkins, R. P., & Dobes, R. W. (1977). Behavioral definitions in applied behavior analysis: Explicit or implicit. In B. C. Etzel, J. M. LeBlanc, & D. M. Baer (Eds.), *New developments in behavioral research: Theory, method, and application* (pp. 167–188). Hillsdale, NJ: Erlbaum.

Homans, G. C. (1950). *The human group.* New York: Harcourt Brace.

Idol, L., Paolucci-Whitcomb, P., & Nevin, A. (1986). *Collaborative consultation.* Rockville, MD: Aspen.

Jayaratne, S., & Levy, R. O. (1979). *Empirical clinical practice.* New York: Columbia University Press.

Kazdin, A. E. (1980). Acceptability of alternative treatments for deviant child behavior. *Journal of Applied Behavior Analysis, 13,* 259–273.

Kazdin, A. E. (1982). *Single-case research designs: Methods for clinical and applied settings.* New York: Oxford University Press.

Kazdin, A. E. (1989). *Behavior modification in applied settings* (rev. ed.). Homewood, IL: Dorsey.

Kazdin, A. E., & Hersen, M. (1980). The current status of behavior therapy. *Behavior Modification, 4,* 283–302.

Kratochwill, T. R. (Ed.). (1978). *Single subject research: Strategies for evaluating change.* New York: Academic Press.

Kratochwill, T. R., & Bergan, J. R. (1978). Evaluating programs in applied settings through behavioral consultation. *Journal of School Psychology, 16,* 375–386.

Kurpius, D., & Robinson, S. E. (1978). Overview of consultation. *Personnel and Guidance Journal, 56,* 321–323.

LaVigna, G. W., & Donnellan, A. M. (1986). *Alternatives to punishment: Solving behavior problems with non-aversive strategies.* New York: Irvington.

Lewin, K. (1951). *Field theory in social science.* New York: Harper.

Lippitt, G. L. (1969). *Organizational renewal.* New York: Appleton-Century-Crofts.

Martens, B. K., & Witt, J. C. (1982). *The Intervention Rating Profile.* Lincoln: University of Nebraska–Lincoln.

Martens, B. K., Witt, J. C., Elliott, S. N., & Darveaux, D. X. (1985). Teacher judgments concerning the acceptability of school-based interventions. *Professional Psychology: Research and Practice, 16*, 191–198.

McNamara, J. R., & Diehl, L. A. (1974). Behavioral consultation with a head start program. *Journal of Community Psychology, 2*, 352–357.

Meyers, J., Parsons, R. D., & Martin, R. (1979). *Mental health consultation in the schools*. San Francisco: Jossey-Bass.

Morris, R. J. (1985). *Behavior modification with children: A systematic guide*. Glenview, IL: Scott Foresman.

Neel, R. S. (1981). How to put the consultant to work in consulting teaching. *Behavioral Disorders, 6*, 82–91.

President's Commission on Mental Health. (1978). *Report to the President* (Vols. 1–4). Washington, DC: U.S. Government Printing Office.

Reschly, D. J. (1976). School psychology consultation: "Frenzied, faddish, or fundamental?" *Journal of School Psychology, 14*, 105–113.

Rogers, C. R. (1942). *Counseling and psychotherapy*. Boston: Houghton Mifflin.

Rogers, C. R. (1951). *Client centered therapy*. Boston: Houghton Mifflin.

Rogers, C. R. (1959). A theory of therapy, personality and interpersonal relationships, as developed in the client-centered framework. In S. Koch (Ed.), *Psychology: A study of science: Vol. II. Formulations of the personal and social concept*. New York: McGraw-Hill.

Rosenfield, S. (1985). Teacher acceptance of behavioral principles: An issue of values. *Teacher Education and Special Education, 8*, 153–137.

Sarason, S. B. (1982). *The culture of the school and the problem of change* (2nd ed.). Boston: Allyn & Bacon.

Schein, E. H. (1969). *Process consultation: Its role in organizational development*. Reading, MA: Addison-Wesley.

Schmuck, R. A. (1982). Organization development in the schools. In C. R. Reynolds & T. B. Gutkin (Eds.), *Handbook of school psychology*. New York: Plenum Press.

Schmuck, R. A., & Miles, M. (1971). *Organization development in the schools*. Palo Alto, CA: National Press Books.

Schmuck, R. A., & Runkel, P. J. (1972). Organizational training. In R. A. Schmuck (Ed.), *Handbook of organizational development in schools*. Palo Alto, CA: Mayfield.

Schwitzgabel, R. L., & Schwitzgabel, M. J. (1980). *Law and psychological practice*. New York: Wiley.

Stokes, T. F., & Baer, D. M. (1977). An implicit technology of generalization. *Journal of Applied Behavior Analysis, 10*, 349–367.

Stolz, S. B., & Associates. (1978). *Ethical issues in behavior modification*. San Francisco: Jossey-Bass.

Sulzer-Azaroff, B., & Mayer, R. G. (1977). *Applying behavior-analysis procedures with children and youth*. New York: Holt, Rinehart, & Winston.

Tharp, R. G., & Wetzel, R. J. (1969). *Behavioral modification in the natural environment*. New York: Academic Press.

Tombari, M. L., & Bergan, J. R. (1978). Consultant cues and teacher verbalizations, judgments and expectations concerning children's adjustment problems. *Journal of School Psychology, 16*, 212–219.

von Bertalanffy, L. (1950). The theory of open systems in physics and biology. *Science, 111*, 23–28.

West, F. J., & Idol, L. (1987). School consultation: 1. An interdisciplinary perspective on theory, models, and research. *Journal of Learning Disabilities, 20*, 388–408.

Witt, J. C., & Elliott, S. N. (1985). Acceptability of classroom intervention strategies. In T. R. Kratochwill (Ed.), *Advances in school psychology* (Vol. 4, pp. 251–288). Hillsdale, NJ: Erlbaum.

Witt, J. C., & Martens, B. K. (1983). Assessing the acceptability of behavioral interventions used in classrooms. *Psychology in the Schools, 20,* 510–517.

Witt, J. C., & Martens, B. K. (1988). Problems with problem-solving consultation: A re-analysis of assumptions, methods, and goals. *School Psychology Review, 17,* 211–226.

Index